THE REAL ONES

By Waleed Akhtar

The Real Ones premiered at the Bush Theatre,
London, on 6 September 2024.

THE REAL ONES
by Waleed Akhtar

Cast

Zaid	Nathaniel Curtis
Neelam	Mariam Haque
Jeremy	Anthony Howell
Deji	Nnabiko Ejimofor

Creative Team

Director	Anthony Simpson-Pike
Set & Costume Designer	Anisha Fields
Lighting Designer	Christoper Nairne
Sound Designer & Composer	Xana
Movement Director	Iskandar Sharazuddin
Video Designer	Matt Powell
Dramaturg	Titilola Dawudu
Casting Director	Jatinder Chera
Costume Supervisor	Maariyah Sharjil
Voice & Accent Coach	Gurkiran Kaur
Intimacy Director	Robbie Taylor Hunt
Assistant Director	Ashen Gupta
Production Dramatherapy	Wabriya King
Production Manager	James Dawson
Company Stage Manager	Rebecca Natalini
Assistant Stage Manager	Rhea Cosford
Production Carpenter	Jay Williamson

This production is generously supported by
Charles Holloway OBE.

CAST

Nathaniel Curtis | Zaid

Nathaniel Curtis is best known for his breakout role of Ash Mukherjee in Russell T Davies' powerful Channel 4 series, *It's A Sin*.

Nathaniel's theatre credits include: *2:22: A Ghost Story* (UK tour); *Disruption* (Park); *Romeo and Juliet* (UK tour); *The Tempest* (UK tour); *Pride and Prejudice* (Regent's Park Open Air Theatre).

On television he has appeared as Brían in *The Witcher: Blood Origin* (Netflix); Dolph Laserhawk in *Captain Laserhawk: A Blood Dragon Remix* (Netflix) and Isaac Newton in *Doctor Who* (BBC).

His audio credits include: *Torchwood – Cuckoo* (Big Finish) and *Auris* (Audible).

Mariam Haque | Neelam

Theatre credits include: *When Winston Went to War with the Wireless* (Donmar Warehouse); *FuN, The House of Bilquis Bibi* (Hampstead Theatre); *The Living Newspaper* (Royal Court); *When the Crows Visit* (Kiln); *Romeo and Juliet, Macbeth* (RSC); *Hometruths* (Cardboard Citizens); *Diana of Dobsons* (New Vic); *Dara, Behind the Beautiful Forevers* (National Theatre); *Almost Near & Hurried Steps* (Finborough); *Crossed Keys* (Eastern Angles); *Invasion?* (Tooting Arts Club); *Monster Under the Bed* (Polka).

Her film and television credits include: *Joy, Black Mirror, Shut Up & Dance* (Netflix); *Such Brave Girls, Ladhood, Worzel Gummidge, This Is Going To Hurt, Henpocalypse!, Pls Like, Doctors, EastEnders, Holby City, Hunted* (BBC); *Live at the Moth Club* (Dave); *What's Happening?* (Baby Cow); *Plebs, The Finale, Midsomer Murders, Finding Alice* (ITV); *What's Love Got To Do With It?* (Studio Canal/Working Title); *Down from London* (Topic); *Trying* (Apple); *Homeland* (Showtime); *Flowers* (Channel 4); *Benjamin, Wasteland* (Open Palm Films); *Smear* (Shadowhouse).

Anthony Howell | Jeremy

Theatre work includes: *King Lear* (Chichester Festival Theatre/ATG); *The Best Man* (Bill Kenwright Ltd); *The Heresy of Love, Julius Caesar, Anne Boleyn, Henry VIII* (Shakespeare's Globe); *The Seagull* (Southwark Playhouse); *Jingo* (Primavera); *A Doll's House, Portrait of a Lady* (Theatre Royal Bath); *The French Lieutenant's Woman* (Nick Brooke Ltd); *The Lifeblood* (Lifeblood Theatre Company); *And Then There Were None* (Act Productions); *Romeo and Juliet, The Comedy of Errors, As You Like It* (RSC); *The Geometry of Miracles* (Ex Machina); *The Promise* (Dalia Ibelhauptaite).

On television he has appeared in: *A Thousand Blows* (Disney+); *Fool Me Once* (Quay Street Pictures/Netflix); *This Town* (Kudos/BBC); *Outlander* (Sony/Starz/Leftbank); *This*

England (Revolutions Films/Sky); *Ransom* (CBS); *Luther, Wives and Daughters* (BBC); *Medici – Kingdom of Gold* (Lux Vide/Big Light Productions); *Apocalypse Slough* (Working Title/NBC for Sky); *Crossing Lines* (NBC); *Dracula* (Sky/NBC); *Dirk Gently* (ITV Productions for BBC4); *Mr Selfridge, Shetland, Foyle's War,* Frances Fyfield's *Helen West, Ultimate Force* (ITV); *Hawking, The Other Boleyn Girl* (BBC Films); *Swallow* (Channel 4).

On film he has appeared in: *Diamond Sky* (Fortunes Cap Productions); *Widow's Walk* (In Your Face Films); *Woman In Gold* (Origin Productions); *Dungeons & Dragons 3: The Book Of Vile Darkness* (Silver Pictures).

Nnabiko Ejimofor | Deji

Nnabiko trained at RADA and received an Olivier Award Nomination for Best Supporting Actor for his performance in *For Black Boys Who Considered Suicide When The Hue Got Too Heavy*, and he won the 2022 Stage Debut Award for Best Performer in a Play.

Recent credits include: *Now, I See* (Stratford East); *Jitney* (Old Vic/Headlong); *For Black Boys Who Considered Suicide When The Hue Got Too Heavy* (West End/Royal Court/New Diorama).

Radio includes: *Sarah Walker's Sunday Morning Show*. Short film credits include: *Good Vibes Only* and *Figure*.

Nnabiko has previously been a dancer for Boy Blue Entertainment and won the Lilian Baylis Award.

CREATIVE TEAM

Waleed Akhtar | Writer

Waleed Akhtar is a writer and actor. He was the recipient of the 2023 Peggy Ramsay/Film 4 bursary and was awarded an MGC Futures bursary in 2021. He won Most Promising Playwright at The Offies 2023 and was nominated for the equivalent at The Evening Standard Theatre Awards. His play, *The P Word*, won the Outstanding Achievement in an Affiliate Theatre at the 2023 Olivier Awards, alongside a nomination for Best Play at the WGGB Awards in 2022.

Work for theatre includes: *The P Word* (Bush); *Kabul Goes Pop: Music Television Afghanistan* (Brixton House/Mercury/HighTide); *Sholay on the Big Screen* (Off Stage Theatre, Bush & Nubian Life); *I Don't Know What To Do* (co-creator – VAULT).

His translation work includes: Alexis Michalik's *The Art of Illusion* (Hampstead Theatre); *Famalam* (Season 4 contributor); *Sketchtopia, Newsjack* (BBC Radio 4 – contributor); *Lost Paradise* (short film, B3 Media/UK Film Council).

He is currently under commission at the Almeida Theatre and Unicorn Theatre.

Work for television includes: *The Road Trip* (Paramount+/42MP) and a television adaptation of his hit play *The P Word* (House Productions). He is a current participant of the BBC Studios

Spotlight scheme developing an original drama with Sid Gentle Films. His original audio play *Mrs Bibi* will be released by Audible in 2025.

As an actor his credits include *Cruella*, *Salmon Fishing in the Yemen* and *The Great*.

Anthony Simpson-Pike | Director

Anthony Simpson-Pike is a director, dramaturg and writer. He was Deputy Artistic Director at the Yard Theatre, Resident Director at Theatre Peckham and Associate Director at the Gate Theatre.

Recent directorial work includes: *Samuel Takes a Break* (Yard); *Beautiful Thing* (Stratford East); *Grenfell: In the Words of Survivors* (National Theatre – transferred to St Ann's Warehouse in New York in April 2024); Olivier Award-winning *The P Word* and *Lava* (nominated for Best Director at the Black British Theatre Awards) (both Bush); *An Octoroon* (Abbey, Dublin – nominated for Best Production, Irish Times Theatre Awards).

Recent dramaturgical credits include: *Now, I See* (Stratford East); *Much Ado About Nothing* (RSC); *Samskara* (Yard); *Hotline* with Produced Moon (Tron); *Dear Young Monster* by Pete McHale (The Queer House); *Coup de Grace* (Royal Court).

Anisha Fields | Set & Costume Designer

Anisha Fields is a set and costume designer, and graduate of the Bristol Old Vic Theatre School. She was the recipient of the Leverhulme Arts Scholarship, resident at the RSC 2018–2019. She was named as one of the Guardian's 12 Theatre Stars to Watch, and was a finalist for Told by an Idiot's Naomi Wilkinson Award 2019. She is an Associate Artist at Theatr Iolo.

Theatre includes: *English* (RSC/Kiln); *The Limit* (Linbury, Royal Opera House); *Some Demon* (Arcola/Bristol Old Vic); *Octopolis*, *Blackout Songs* (Hampstead Theatre); *Mom, How Did You Meet The Beatles?* (Chichester Festival Theatre); *Squirrel* (Unicorn/Mac/The Egg/Bath Theatre Royal); *Pandemonium* (Soho Theatre); *Wendy* (The Egg/Bath Theatre Royal); *Walworth Farce* (Southwark Playhouse); *Kes* (Bolton Octagon/Theatre By The Lake); *Owl at Home* (Theatre Iolo).

Christopher Nairne | Lighting Designer

Christopher Nairne was awarded OffWestEnd.com's Best Lighting Designer Award in 2016 for *Teddy* at Southwark Playhouse. He was recently shortlisted at the inaugural Profile Awards for his work on *Blackout Songs* at Hampstead Theatre.

Other theatre includes: Mischief Theatre's *Groan Ups* (West End & UK tour); *Boy Parts*, *Chasing*

Bono (Soho Theatre); *Tom Fool, Mayfly* (Orange Tree); *Samuel Takes a Break, This Beautiful Future* (Yard); *Infamous* (Jermyn Street); *Jeeves & Wooster in Perfect Nonsense, The Last Temptation of Boris Johnson* (UK tours); *Suzy Storck* (Gate/France tour); *Preludes* (Southwark Playhouse); *The Legend of Sleepy Hollow, The Beautiful Game, A Little Princess* (Other Palace); *Jerusalem* (Watermill); *Speech & Debate, BU21* (Trafalgar Studios); Complicité's *Lionboy* (world tour).

Opera work includes: *L'Agrippina* (Barber Opera); *Madame Butterfly, Jephtha, Macbeth* (Iford Arts); *Belshazzar* (Trinity Laban); *Vivienne* (Linbury, Royal Opera House); *La Bohème* (OperaUpClose, 2011 Olivier Award Winner).

Xana | Sound Designer & Composer

Xana is a freestyle live loop musician, composer, spatial sound artist, music supervisor and a haptic specialist sound designer developing accessible audio systems for live art spaces. Xana is the music science and technology lead and project mentor supporting artists and inventors at audio research label Inventing Waves.

Recent credits include: *Dead Girls Rising* (Silent Uproar, UK tour); *Shifters* (also West End), *Elephant, Sleepova* (Olivier Award), *The P Word* (Olivier Award), *Strange Fruit* (all Bush); *The Architect* (ATC/GDIF);

Beautiful Thing (Stratford East); *Imposter 22, Word:Play, Living Newspaper #4* (Royal Court); *Anna Karenina* (Edinburgh Lyceum/Bristol Old Vic); *The Trials, Marys Seacole* (Donmar Warehouse); *Earthworks, Sundown Kiki: Reloaded, The Collaboration, Sundown Kiki, Changing Destiny, Fairview, Ivan and the Dogs* (Young Vic); *...cake* (Theatre Peckham); *Who Killed My Father* (Tron); *as british as a watermelon* (Contact); *Hyde and Seek* (Guildhall); *Burgerz* (Hackney Showroom); *King Troll [The Fawn]* (New Diorama); *Everyday* (Deafinitely); *Black Holes* (The Place); *Hive City Legacy* (Roundhouse); *Glamrou: From Quran to Queen, Curious, Half-Breed* (Soho Theatre); *Blood Knot, Guards at the Taj* (Orange Tree); *Main Character Energy, Samuel Takes a Break, SEX SEX MEN MEN* (Yard); *Everything I Own, Is Dat Yu Yeah* (Brixton House).

Xana is the recipient of the 2023 Best Sound Design award from the Black British Theatre Awards (BBTA).

Iskandar Sharazuddin | Movement Director

Iskandar Sharazuddin is a theatre artist, Associate at Headlong and the Joint Artistic Director of Ellandar Productions, a British East and Southeast Asian theatre company.

Selected credits as Movement Director: *King Troll [The Fawn]* (New Diorama); *The Bleeding Tree* (Southwark Playhouse –

Nominated Best Movement/ Choreography, Off West End Awards); *Liberation Squares* (Nottingham/Brixton House/UK tour – Nominated Best Ensemble, Off West End Awards); *The Garden of Words* (Park); *Worth* (New Earth/ Storyhouse Live/Arcola); *A Play for the Living in a Time of Extinction* (Headlong/Barbican); *Blackout Songs* (Hampstead Theatre – Nominated Achievement in Affiliate Theatre, Olivier Awards); *Satyagraha, Così fan tutte* (English National Opera).

As Dance-Dramaturg & Puppetry Director: *(un)written • (un)heard* (Fringe World Festival Western Australia – Winner: International Dance & Physical Theatre Award).

As Associate Movement Director: *The Climbers* (Theatre by the Lake).

Selected credits as a director: *The Lonesome Death of Eng Bunker* (Kakilang/Omnibus); *harmony.* 天人合一 (York Theatre Royal); *Turandot* (Grimeborn Opera Festival – Nominated Best Opera Production & Winner Best Opera Performance, Off West End Awards).

He is the Resident Director & Puppetry Captain of *My Neighbour Totoro* (RSC/ Barbican/West End) and former Resident & Dance Captain on *How To Train Your Dragon: Live* (DreamWorks SKG/Global Creatures).

Matt Powell | Video Designer

Matt Powell (they/she/he) is a non-binary, Offie-finalist video designer, musical-theatre creative and queer practitioner based in the East Midlands. They are a PhD candidate exploring LGBTQ+ representation in musical theatre at the University of Wolverhampton.

Video design and digital credits include: *New Year* (Birmingham Opera); *Marie Curie – A New Musical*, *Rebecca* (Charing Cross); *Laughing Boy* (Jermyn Street/Theatre Royal Bath); *Sherlock Holmes and the Poison Wood* (Watermill); *EXhibitionists* (King's Head); *I Really Do Think That This Will Change Your Life* (Mercury/Colchester – Finalist The Stage Award for Innovation): *Gypsy in Concert* (Manchester Opera House for Hope Mill Theatre); *Ride* (The Old Globe/Curve/Southwark Playhouse); *Animal* (Hope Mill/ Park – Offie Finalist); *Accidental Death of an Anarchist* (Theatre Royal Haymarket/Sheffield/Lyric Hammersmith); *Blow Down* (Leeds Playhouse); *Rumi: The Musical* (Badhri Performing Arts Festival/London Coliseum); *How A City Can Save the World* (Sheffield); *A-Typical Rainbow* (Turbine); *Flight* (RCM); *But What If You Die* (Camden People's Theatre); *Old Friends* (Digital Theatre); *Bloody Difficult Women* (Riverside); *Santa Must Die* (Alphabetti); *Magdalene* (Arcola Outside); *Snowflake* (Lowry); *34* (Aria Entertainment/Lowry); *Public Domain* (Vaudeville/Southwark Playhouse); *The Blazing World*

(University of the Arts, Philadelphia); *On Hope: A Digital Song Cycle* (Other Palace); *Plaza* (Royal Central School of Speech and Drama); *American Idiot* (Derby).

Directing credits include: *Rent* (May Hall); *Santa Must Die* (Leeds Playhouse/Red Ladder); *Nativity: The Musical, Crazy for You* (Derby); *The Unconventionals* (VAULT); *Is He Musical* (Curve/Other Palace).

Titilola Dawudu | Dramaturg

Titilola Dawudu is the Associate Dramaturg at the Bush Theatre, heading up the Literary department. She works with the Artistic Director and Associate Artistic Director to commission and nurture news plays and ideas, working closely with writers, managing writing groups and the talent development pipeline.

Titilola was the dramaturg for an early iteration at Ovalhouse of Tyrell Williams's award-winning play *Red Pitch*. She dramaturgically supported some of the RSC's 37 Plays winners, most notably *Dreaming and Drowning* by Kwame Owusu.

Titilola co-created and edited *Hear Me Now: Audition Monologues for Actors of Colour* with Tamasha, published by Oberon Books. *Hear Me Now: Volume Two* was published in August 2022 by Methuen Drama. As a writer, Titilola has written for Theatre Royal Arojah in Abuja, Nigeria, Theatre Peckham, Ovalhouse, Beyond Face and Soho Theatre.

Jatinder Chera | Casting Director

For the Bush: Olivier Award winning *Sleepova* and *The P Word*, and Olivier Award-nominated *A Playlist for The Revolution*.

Theatre includes: *G* (Royal Court); *The Comeuppance* (Almeida); *The Flea, Samuel Takes a Break, Multiple Casualty Incident* (Yard); *Sweat* (Royal Exchange, Manchester).

Maariyah Sharjil | Costume Supervisor

Maariyah Sharjil is a designer and recent first-class graduate from BA Design for Performance at the Royal Central School of speech and Drama. Before her design training, Maariyah worked at Sands Films as a costume constructor.

Her most recent productions include: Costume Researcher for *Life of Pi* (American Repertory Theatre); Design Associate and Costume Supervisor for *The P Word* (Bush – Olivier Award); Assistant Costume Supervisor for *The Father and the Assassin* (National); Costume Designer for *The Key Workers' Cycle* (Almeida).

She has a passion for detailed research and often has an expansive reading list that inspires her work. The heart of her practice is turning the stories of minority communities and the diaspora into a visual language while also embedding historical and cultural themes into her work and designs.

Gurkiran Kaur | Voice & Accent Coach

Gurkiran Kaur is a voice, accent and dialect coach from London. She holds a BA Drama and Theatre Studies (Royal Holloway), completed actor training (The Bridge Theatre Training Company) and has a MA Voice Studies (The Royal Central School of Speech and Drama). Gurkiran works at a number of drama schools and has coached a number of graduate productions and showcases. Gurkiran is part of The Voice and Speech Teaching Associations' EduCore Leadership Team and serves as a Junior Board Member. Gurkiran honours Ancient practices to approach voice work and believes in serving the people in the space ensuring inclusivity, equity and accessibility.

Credits: *Extinct* (Stratford East); *Queens of Sheba* (Soho Theatre/ Nouveau Riche); *NW Trilogy* (Kiln); *How To Save The Planet When You're A Young Carer And Broke* (Boundless); *Best of Enemies* (Young Vic & Headlong); *Chasing Hares* (Young Vic)' Uncut); *I Wonder If* (Young Vic), *Red Pitch, Favour, The P Word, Paradise Now!, Sleepova, A Playlist For The Revolution, The Cord* (Bush); *Lotus Beauty* (Hampstead Theatre/Tamasha); *Henry VIII* (Shakespeare's Globe); *Offside* (Futures Theatre); *Marvin's Binoculars, Anansi The Spider* (Unicorn); *The Climbers* (Theatre by the Lake); *Finding Home* (Curve); *The Best Exotic Marigold Hotel* (Noël Coward); *Silence* (Donmar Warehouse/

Tara); *A Dead Body In Taos* (Fuel); *Unexpected Twist* (Royal & Derngate); *Wuthering Heights* (China Plate); *I Wanna Be Yours* (Melbourne Theatre Company); *The Empress, Falkland Sound* (RSC); *Brassic FM* (Gate); *A Poem for Rabia* (Tarragon Theatre, Toronto); *The Full Monty* (Everyman, Cheltenham/Buxton Opera House); *Good Karma Hospital* (ITV & Tiger Aspect Productions) and *Hotel Portofino* (ITV, PBS & Eagle Eye).

Robbie Taylor Hunt | Intimacy Director

Robbie Taylor Hunt is an intimacy director & coordinator and theatre-maker.

As an intimacy coordinator he has worked on productions for Netflix, HBO, Disney, Paramount, Amazon Prime Video, the BBC, Channel 4, ITV and Apple TV.

Recent TV credits include: *Big Boys* (Channel 4); *Mary & George* (Sky); *You* Season 4 (Netflix); *Mr Loverman* (BBC Studios) Film credits Include: *Femme, Pearl* and *Red, White and Royal Blue.*

As a theatre-maker, he recently co-created *Pansexual Pregnant Piracy* and *Lesbian Space Crime* (Soho Theatre).

Ashen Gupta | Assistant Director

Ashen Gupta (they/them) is a director, facilitator and musician, whose work spans new writing for the stage, opera and short film. Much of their work is political in nature and has a focus on marginalised communities (particularly those of the South Asian diaspora and the queer community) as well as having musical elements.

Theatre includes: *Brown Sheep* (VAULT); *Chasing Hares, Khab Jeetigi* (Young Vic); *Jack and the Beanstalk* (Stratford East); *Laughing Boy* (Jermyn Street/ Theatre Royal Bath); *NW Trilogy* (Kiln); *Pygmalion* (Lyric Hammersmith).

Opera includes: *Carmen, Gloriana* (London Coliseum); *The Promise Opera* (UK tour).

Short film includes: *I Threw It* (Old Vic); *JINEOLOGÎ* (Shoreditch Town Hall); *Living Newspaper* (Royal Court); *TWENTYTWENTY* (Young Vic).

Wabriya King | Production Dramatherapy

Wabriya King is the Associate Dramatherapist at the Bush Theatre. Wabriya's practice is to create a space and a format to hold people safely while they navigate their experiences in relation to the theatre's work. Wabriya has previously worked on productions at Soho Theatre, Theatre Royal Stratford East, Hampstead Theatre, Royal Court, National Theatre and Paines Plough.

Credits for the Bush include: *My Father's Fable; Shifters* (also West End); *Paradise Now!, The P Word, House of Ife, Red Pitch, Overflow, Lava, The High Table.*

James Dawson | Production Manager

James Dawson is a freelance production manager for theatre, opera and dance working across London, nationally and internationally with a passion for touring work, performance art and community projects.

Recent projects include: interactive children's play space *REPLAY* (Southbank Centre); *A View from the Bridge* (Headlong); *Love & Rebellion Festival* (Birmingham Rep); Marikiscrycrycry's *GONER* (global tour).

James has worked as a production manager with Young Vic Theatre, Unicorn Theatre, Hampstead Theatre, Battersea Arts Centre, Bush Theatre, Pace Live entertainment, National Youth Theatre, Chichester Festival Theatre and The Yard Theatre.

Rebecca Natalini | Company Stage Manager

Rebecca Natalini graduated with a BA in Stage Management from the Royal Central School of Speech and Drama and she is very excited to be working at the Bush Theatre for the first time.

Recent stage management theatre credits include: *Pride and Prejudice, Scenes from RENT – A Staged Performance* (Curve); *A Midsummer Night's Dream* (New Diorama): *Zoe's Peculiar Journey Through Time* (UK and Norway tour); *Pride & Prejudice* (*sort of)* (UK tour).

Rhea Cosford | Assistant Stage Manager

Rhea Cosford studied Drama at Queen Mary University of London before going on to train in Stage and Events Management at Royal Welsh College of Music and Drama.

Stage management theatre credits include: *2:22: A Ghost Story* (Criterion); *Trade* (Pleasance); *Walk Right Back – The Everly Brothers Story* (UK tour); *Phantasmagoria* (Kali/ Southwark Playhouse); *What Would Jarvis Do?* (Omnibus); *Multiple Casualty Incident* (Yard).

Bush Theatre

We make theatre for London. Now.

For over 50 years the Bush Theatre has been a world-famous home for new plays and an internationally renowned champion of playwrights.

Combining ambitious artistic programming with meaningful community engagement work and industry leading talent development schemes, the Bush Theatre champions and supports unheard voices to develop the artists and audiences of the future.

Since opening in 1972 the Bush has produced more than 500 ground-breaking premieres of new plays, developing an enviable reputation for its acclaimed productions nationally and internationally.

They have nurtured the careers of writers including James Graham, Lucy Kirkwood, Temi Wilkey, Jonathan Harvey and Jack Thorne. Recent successes include Tyrell Williams' *Red Pitch*, Benedict Lombe's *Shifters*, and Arinzé Kene's *Misty*. The Bush has won over 100 awards including the Olivier Award for Outstanding Achievement in Affliate Theatre for the past four years for Richard Gadd's *Baby Reindeer*, Igor Memic's *Old Bridge*, Waleed Akhtar's *The P Word* and Matilda Feyiṣayọ Ibini's *Sleepova*.

Located in the renovated old library on Uxbridge Road in the heart of Shepherd's Bush, the Bush Theatre continues to create a space where all communities can be part of its future and call the theatre home.

'The place to go for ground-breaking work as diverse as its audiences' EVENING STANDARD

bushtheatre.co.uk
@bushtheatre

Artistic Director	Lynette Linton
Executive Director	Mimi Findlay
Associate Artistic Director	Daniel Bailey
Deputy Executive Director	Angela Wachner
Development & Marketing Assistant	Nicima Abdi
Development Officer	Laura Aiton
Head of Marketing	Shannon Clarke
Head of Development	Jocelyn Cox
Associate Dramaturg	Titilola Dawudu
Finance Assistant	Lauren Francis
Resident Director & Young Company Director	Katie Greenall
Technical & Buildings Manager	Jamie Haigh
Assistant Venue Manager	Rae Harm
Head of Finance	Neil Harris
Marketing Officer	Laela Henley-Rowe
Associate Producer	Nikita Karia
Community Assistant	Joanne Leung
Senior Producer	Oscar Owen
Assistant Venue Manager	Simon Pilling
Senior Technician	John Pullig
Event Sales Manager & Technician	Charlie Sadler
Venue Manager (Theatre)	Ade Seriki
Press Manager	Martin Shippen
Community Producer	Holly Smith
Literary & Producing Assistant	Laetitia Somè
Marketing Manager	Ed Theakston
Assistant Venue Manager (Box Office)	Robin Wilks
Theatre Administrator & Executive Assistant	Chloe Wilson
Café Bar Manager	Wayne Wilson

DUTY MANAGERS
Sara Dawood, Molly Elson, Thomas Ingram, Madeleine Simpson-Kent &
Anna-May Wood.

VENUE SUPERVISORS
Antony Dakin, Addy Caulder-James, Stephanie Cremona, Emma Chatel,
Zea Hilland, Nzuzi Malemda, Roy Mas, Jacob Meier & Louis Nicholson.

VENUE ASSISTANTS
Javine Aduganfi, Doridan Bavangila, Charlotte Binns, Will Byam-Shaw,
Pyerre Clarke, Daniel Fesoom, Matias Hailu, Bo Leandro, Maya Li Preti,
Ishani McGuire, Khy Matinez, April Miller, Ed Mendoza, Carys Murray, Chana
Nardone, Jennifer Okolo, James Robertson, Ali Shah & Nefertari Williams.

BOARD OF TRUSTEES
Uzma Hasan (Chair), Mark Dakin, Kim Evans, Keerthi Kollimada,
Lynette Linton, Anthony Marraccino, Jim Marshall, Rajiv Nathwani,
Kwame Owusu, Stephen Pidcock, Catherine Score & Cllr Mercy Umeh.

Bush Theatre, 7 Uxbridge Road, London W12 8LJ
Box Office: 020 8743 5050 | Administration: 020 8743 3584
Email: info@bushtheatre.co.uk | bushtheatre.co.uk

Alternative Theatre Company Ltd
The Bush Theatre is a Registered Charity
and a company limited by guarantee.
Registered in England no. 1221968 Charity no. 270080

THANK YOU

Our supporters make our work possible. Together, we're evolving the canon and creating a bolder, more diverse, and representative future for British theatre. We're so grateful to you all.

MAJOR DONORS
Charles Holloway OBE
Jim & Michelle Gibson
Georgia Oetker
Cathy & Tim Score
Susie Simkins
Jack Thorne
Gianni & Michael Alen-Buckley

SHOOTING STARS
Jim & Michelle Gibson
Cathy & Tim Score
Susie Simkins

LONE STARS
Jax & Julian Bull
Clyde Cooper
Adam Kenwright
Anthony Marraccino & Mariela Manso
Jim Marshall
Georgia Oetker

HANDFUL OF STARS
Charlie Bigham
Judy Bollinger
David des Jardins
Sue Fletcher
Elizabeth Jack
Simon & Katherine Johnson
Joanna Kennedy
Garry & Lorna Lawrence
Phyllida Lloyd & Kate Pakenham
Vivienne Lukey
Aditya Mittal
Sam & Jim Murgatroyd
Mark & Anne Paterson
Martha Plimpton

Nick & Annie Reid
Bhagat Sharma
Joe Tinston & Amelia Knott
Dame Emma Thompson

RISING STARS
Elizabeth Beebe
Martin Blackburn
David Brooks
Catharine Browne
Anthony Chantry
Lauren Clancy
Richard & Sarah Clarke
Caroline Clasen
Susan Cuff
Matthew Cushen
Anne-Hélène and Rafaël Biosse Duplan
Austin Erwin
Kim Evans
Mimi Findlay
Jack Gordon
Hugh & Sarah Grootenhuis
Thea Guest
Sarah Harrison
Uzma Hasan
Lesley Hill & Russ Shaw
Davina & Malcolm Judelson
Mike Lewis
Lynette Linton
Michael McCoy
Judy Mellor
Caro Millington
Rajiv Nathwani
Yoana Nenova
Stephen Pidcock
Miguel & Valeri Ramos Handal
Karen & John Seal

James St. Ville KC
Jan Topham
Kit & Anthony van Tulleken
Evanna White
Ben Yeoh

CORPORATE SPONSORS
Biznography
Casting Pictures Ltd.
Nick Hern Books
S&P Global
The Agency

TRUSTS & FOUNDATIONS
Backstage Trust
Buffini Chao Foundation
Christina Smith Foundation
Daisy Trust
Esmée Fairbairn Foundation
The Foyle Foundation
Garfield Weston Foundation
Garrick Charitable Trust
Hammersmith United Charities
The Harold Hyam Wingate Foundation
Idlewild Trust
Jerwood Foundation
Martin Bowley Charitable Trust
Noël Coward Foundation
The Thistle Trust

And all the donors who wish to remain anonymous.

If you are interested in finding out how to be involved, please visit **bushtheatre.co.uk/support-us** email **development@bushtheatre.co.uk** or call **020 8743 3584**.

THE REAL ONES

Waleed Akhtar

To all the women
I've ever called a friend

Characters

NEELAM, *female, British Pakistani, straight. Formidable.*
  Plays nineteen to late thirties
ZAID, *male, British Pakistani, queer. Radiates a queer energy.*
  Plays nineteen to late thirties
JEREMY, *male, white, queer. Privileged. Plays fifties to sixties*
DEJI, *male, British Nigerian, straight. Intelligent. Plays late*
  twenties to mid-thirties

*The play charts the course of Neelam and Zaid's friendship
from when they are nineteen to thirty-six. Starting in 2006 and
ending in the present day.*

*This text went to press before the end of rehearsals and so may
differ slightly from the play as performed.*

A memory. Which disintegrates more each time we visit it.
Elements getting stripped away, including the words.

Club. High off their faces. An indie classic plays.

NEELAM. Can you feel anything?

ZAID. Yeah. Yeah. Can you?

NEELAM. Yeah.

ZAID. Yeah!

They both uncontrollably laugh.

I love you. Like genuinely I love you.

NEELAM. I love you too.

ZAID. No really, I love the bones of you.

NEELAM. What?

ZAID. I LOVE THE BONES OF YOU.

Beat.

NEELAM. I love the skin of you.

ZAID. The teeth of you

NEELAM. The eyes.

ZAID. The ears.

NEELAM. The nose.

A moment of intense connection.

You know we're gonna be fine.

ZAID. We're gonna be fucking brilliant.

19

Zaid's university accommodation.

NEELAM *is flashing her bra out the window.*

ZAID. I dared you to flash your tits. That's just your bra.

NEELAM. You mad, bruv. The sight of these bad girls are worth a million each.

ZAID. Rupees? SHOT!

NEELAM *takes a swig of a drink.*

NEELAM. This is lame.

ZAID. No it's not?

NEELAM. Did not come all this way to play Truth or Dare. You're not even drinking.

ZAID. I don't like it.

NEELAM. You've only tried it once. Zaid, I beg, don't be a pussyhole this weekend.

ZAID. I don't need to drink to have fun.

NEELAM. Stop acting all pious. Literally sat in the toilet of a fucking train to get here.

ZAID. You could have bought a ticket like a normal person.

NEELAM. Fuck that, have you seen how much they cost? You're so lucky living out at uni. Some of us were forced to stay at home.

ZAID. Living out isn't all it's cracked up to be. Everyone is so posh.

NEELAM. Everyone at school thought you were hella posh.

ZAID. That's because no one we went to school with had ever left Ilford.

NEELAM. True. But you escaped Mini-Pakistan.

ZAID. No one cool does computer science.

NEELAM. Join the theatre society.

ZAID. Too cliquey... And none of them are into writing.

NEELAM. I went.

ZAID. Got no motivation, barely keeping up with my course.

NEELAM. You'll make friends.

ZAID. Mates maybe. Friends, I don't know, takes me a while.

NEELAM. If they can't see how great you are, fuck 'em. I'm
your people. You know that, right?!

ZAID. Yes. Right, my turn, Truth or Dare.

NEELAM. We still doing this? Already know what you're
gonna say.

ZAID. Truth.

NEELAM. Why? Every time.

ZAID. Then just ask me something you've always wanted to
ask me?

NEELAM. I don't know what to ask.

ZAID. Just ask me.

NEELAM. Ask you what, Zaid?

They both clock each other.

Why don't you just say what you want to say?

ZAID. I've tried. I need you to ask me, might make it easier.

NEELAM. Erm... Tell me something... surprising about you?
Something you've never told anyone.

ZAID. Right. I feel like there was this moment when I should
have told you back in sixth form. When you said no matter
what you'd always have my back. But I didn't. But I should
have. Because I think you were hinting.

So you've probably guessed and you know already.

NEELAM. Is this what I think you're saying?

ZAID. What do you think I'm saying?

NEELAM. Well… What if I'm wrong and you're not saying what I think you're saying?

ZAID. Just say it.

NEELAM. I can't be the one to say it.

ZAID. I'm gay.

Silence.

Well fucking say something.

NEELAM. I said tell me something surprising about you.

ZAID. Fucking cow.

***

Club.

NEELAM. Look, I'm here for you.

ZAID. I can't.

NEELAM. What's the worst that could happen?

ZAID. I don't know?

NEELAM. Seriously go on.

ZAID. I'll go over there and talk to him and he'll laugh at me or just tell me to fuck off.

NEELAM. And the best that could happen?

ZAID. We fall in love and live happily ever after.

NEELAM. So the reality is somewhere in between both those things.

***

Uni accommodation.

ZAID. Do you think everyone at school knew?

NEELAM. I don't know.

ZAID. Real talk.

NEELAM. I think people said things.

ZAID. To you?

NEELAM. Not to me, obviously. I would have fucking battered
'em.

ZAID. What kind of things?

NEELAM. It doesn't matter now. School's over.

ZAID. Please.

NEELAM. Just that you'd never had a girlfriend and you were
a bit… girly.

ZAID. Girly?

NEELAM. You don't like normal boy shit.

ZAID. Football?

NEELAM. And vaginas.

ZAID.

NEELAM. It's not a bad thing. Being gay.

ZAID. Not the greatest thing either. And don't get me started on
the religious stuff.

NEELAM. You're one of the best people I know.

ZAID. What do I do with it?

NEELAM. What do you mean?

ZAID. Do I tell people? My parents would freak. Do I just
marry a woman? Don't want that. Like what the fuck does
my life look like?

NEELAM. What does any of our lives look like?

ZAID. Least you know some things, you'll get married, have kids.

NEELAM. Do I look like I want to become a basic *bushra*
from ends?

ZAID. At least it's there if you want it.

   Beat.

NEELAM. Look, Zaid, all you can do is take it one day at a time.

                              ***

Club.

ZAID. I'm better online.

NEELAM. But you're here now and he's been eyeing you up!

ZAID. Not sure he was.

NEELAM. Want me to go up to him?

ZAID. No.

NEELAM. So go, I'll be right here. GO!

                              ***

Uni accommodation.

ZAID. It feels weird. Having this thing that I held on to, just having it out there.

NEELAM. Chill, bitch. It's me. Always got your back.

ZAID. And I've got yours.

NEELAM. Right, mine's a truth.

ZAID. We don't have to play any more.

NEELAM. Yes we do. Ask me about the rumours from sixth form.

ZAID. Are you sure?

NEELAM. I said ask me.

ZAID. Was the gossip about you and Kasim true?

NEELAM. Yes.

ZAID. Right.

NEELAM. Wanted to tell you for time, but it all got so fucked and at that point you were the only friend I had left. Didn't want to risk it.

ZAID. Sort of guessed you'd slept with him, but I didn't want to ask. Know what it's like people saying things about you behind your back.

NEELAM. Real talk. What exactly would people say about me?

ZAID. Seriously, just the stuff you probably know already. I wasn't popular enough for any of that lot to speak to me. Fuck Kasim for telling everyone.

NEELAM. Said *Walahi* on his mum's life it wasn't him.

ZAID. Who else was it?

NEELAM. I told Rehana as well.

ZAID. What?

NEELAM. She was my best mate at the time. She said she told one person just to get some advice and boom everyone knew and nobody was speaking to me.

ZAID. And you believed her?

NEELAM. I don't know. We stopped talking after that.

ZAID. You were always better than that lot. Rehana is a knob.

NEELAM. Anyway fuck her and fuck school. That was the peak for those losers

ZAID. Fucking losers.

NEELAM. And I'm still stuck in Ilford with most of them.

ZAID. But you're nothing like them. We're going to be famous writers.

NEELAM. Have people read our shit for years to come.

ZAID. While they'll just remain basic.

Beat.

NEELAM. Now we've got no secrets.

ZAID. Actually, I stole the money from Mrs Cook's purse, in Year 9. She was a bitch and it was just there.

NEELAM. We got detention for a month and you never said anything?

ZAID. I was in too deep.

***

Club.

NEELAM. Well what did he say? You were talking for ages.

ZAID. He was cool. Studying music production, was born in Sheffield. Loves the Arctic Monkeys.

NEELAM. Did you get his number?

ZAID. No.

NEELAM. Why not?

ZAID. He's straight.

NEELAM. Fucking straights. They're everywhere.

ZAID. Trust me to hit on the only straight guy here.

NEELAM. You have balls. Fucking went up to someone and chatted them up.

ZAID. Yeah I did it. Should've got his number for you?

NEELAM. Not my type... looks gay.

They laugh.

I'm off boys anyway.

ZAID. Me too now.

NEELAM. No, you can do it again.

ZAID. Not tonight. I think I need a drink.

NEELAM. You don't drink.

ZAID. Good time to give it another go.

NEELAM. Nah. I've got something better.

***

Uni accommodation.

NEELAM. No more moping, let's go out.

ZAID. Don't think I'm in the mood now.

NEELAM. Come on, Zaid. I'm here and we're gonna party like an Asian girl who's told her parents she is at an Islamic conference!!

ZAID. They believed that?

NEELAM. Yep. Printed out a permission slip, like it was junior school or something.

ZAID. Alright then.

NEELAM. Yes, yes. We can go somewhere gay.

ZAID. No.

NEELAM. I've always wanted to be a fag hag. Too soon?

ZAID. Don't know if I'm ready to just go to a gay place.

NEELAM. I dare you.

***

Club.

NELLAM *is offering* ZAID *a pill.*

NEELAM. ZAID!

ZAID. I don't want to.

NEELAM. Zaid, I beg you.

ZAID. What if I die?

NEELAM. You're not going to die.

ZAID. Nah, I'm not doing it.

Indie anthem #2 plays. NEELAM *and* ZAID *are overjoyed.*

NEELAM/ZAID. Yes!

NEELAM. Come on.

ZAID. I can have a good time without it.

NEELAM. But you'll have a better time with it.

ZAID. Just say no.

NEELAM. Yes. Muthafucker. Yes! Just say yes… this is fucking peer pressure.

ZAID. Fine… fine.

NEELAM. Yes!!

ZAID. If I die you have to delete all the gay porn off my laptop and delete my Facebook.

NEELAM. Oh my god you have to do the same for me – delete all my hoe pictures.

ZAID. What if we both die?

NEELAM. Then we're fucked.

They swallow the pills.

***

Uni accommodation. NEELAM *and* ZAID *in bed together.*

NEELAM. Fuck, my head hurts.

ZAID. My jaw hurts.

NEELAM. You were gurning like a muthafucker.

ZAID. It was good though.

NEELAM. Was it now?? Remember, it's a slippery slope… *crack is wack.*

ZAID. Thanks for coming with me and just being cool with everything. I wish you didn't have to leave.

NEELAM. I'll come up again.

ZAID. And how are you going to manage that?

NEELAM. I'm an Asian girl – getting out the house without my
parents suspecting is a super-power. And next time we'll get
you your first boyfriend.

ZAID. I've had a boyfriend before.

NEELAM. It's me, Zaid, you don't have to bullshit now, bro.

ZAID. Not bullshitting.

NEELAM. Okay then.

ZAID. I'm not. Broke up when I got to sixth form, that's why
I would write all that emo poetry.

NEELAM. Really?

ZAID. Yeah really.

NEELAM. You gonna tell me more then?

ZAID. What do you wanna know?

NEELAM. Literally know what you had for breakfast last
week, but when it comes to the good shit you're all stush.

ZAID. Greg. Met him on chat.

NEELAM. Online?

ZAID. Yeah, it was Year 10.

NEELAM. It doesn't count if you never met the guy.

ZAID. We did meet. He would come pick me up after school,

NEELAM. Pick you up?

ZAID. Yeah.

NEELAM. In a car?

ZAID. Yeah. And then we'd usually hang at his.

NEELAM. And how old was he?

ZAID. Thirty-nine when we first met.

NEELAM. And you were in Year 10?

ZAID. Yeah.

Beat.

What?

NEELAM. Nothing.

***

Club. High off their faces. An indie classic plays.

NEELAM. Can you feel anything?

ZAID. Yeah. ▮▮▮▮▮▮▮

NEELAM. Yeah.

ZAID. Yeah!

They both uncontrollably laugh.

I love you. ▮▮▮▮▮▮▮▮▮▮

NEELAM. I love you too.

ZAID. No really, I love the bones of you.

NEELAM. What?

ZAID. I LOVE THE BONES OF YOU.

Beat

NEELAM. I love the skin of you.

ZAID. The teeth of you.

NEELAM. The eyes.

ZAID. The ears.

NEELAM. The nose.

A moment of intense connection.

ZAID. This is forever.

NEELAM. You know we're gonna be fine.

ZAID. We're gonna be fucking brilliant.

24

Cinema – NEELAM *and* ZAID *are cleaning the cinema after a film.*

NEELAM. 'What have been your barriers to the industry and some of the hardships you have faced?'

ZAID. Gay and Muslim should defo get my travel covered right?

NEELAM. What the fuck is that question?

ZAID. I know.

NEELAM. Why does it always feel like that?

ZAID. Because we're poor and we need money.

NEELAM. I didn't bother answering it.

ZAID. Jeremy said I should. At the theatre's open house. He's kind of fit.

NEELAM. Jeremy.

ZAID. Yeah.

NEELAM. Jeremy who's gonna run the writing scheme?

ZAID. Yeah.

NEELAM. Jeremy? The old *gora*.

ZAID. Yes. I find older guys sexy.

NEELAM. You're twenty-four, you should have more confidence, bro.

ZAID. I do. You know he's gay?

NEELAM. Not surprised.

ZAID. He told me, when I was telling him about the play I was going to write and submit – *Diary of a Call Girl* but Asian and gay.

NEELAM. Sounds good… You know people would know if it went on.

ZAID. Most people do. I'm defo going to put on the application form, for the bursary thing.

NEELAM. I'll just keep cleaning people's crap off the floor. Like how hard is it to get popcorn in your gob?

ZAID. Last week I found a used condom.

NEELAM. Gross.

ZAID. At least they were responsible.

They laugh and go back to cleaning.

NEELAM. Actually meant your family would know, if they put the play on.

ZAID. Cross that bridge when I come to it.

Sometimes I think my dad might be alright with it. He's always said it's okay to be sensitive. And my mum really likes Graham Norton. But then all of them say off-key things at times.

NEELAM. Swear an uncle of mine is in his fifties and never got married, he must be. Don't see him much any more.

ZAID. My mum asked me if you were my girlfriend.

NEELAM. My parents still think you're a girl too. You'll always be saved as Zainab in my phone.

ZAID. Prefer Xena. Like the warrior princess.

NEELAM. What did you say to your mum then?

ZAID. No, obviously. She wouldn't believe me. Said it was better to get married than to carry on with a girl. I thought little do you know.

NEELAM. You should never have dropped out of uni, you managed to break free. If my parents ever come around to the idea of me moving out, I'm never coming back.

ZAID. Living out wasn't all that, and I hated my course.

NEELAM. Suppose I could do a lot worse than marry you. Asian boys are dicks. Especially if you got a 'reputation', only after one thing.

ZAID. You'll find the right guy.

NEELAM. Why do I need a guy?

ZAID. True. Do you know what you're going to submit, what play you're gonna write?

NEELAM. A story about a girl at school who ruins her 'reputation' for the most underwhelming one minute thirty seconds of her life. Write what you know.

***

Cinema box office.

NEELAM. Fuck, fuck, fuck. I've been looking for you everywhere, what are you doing on box office?

ZAID. Andrew's IBS flared up. Is everything okay?

NEELAM. Kill me now.

ZAID. What?

NEELAM. Rehana was here.

ZAID. No way.

NEELAM. Yeah.

ZAID. What was she doing out of ends?

NEELAM. Came to watch a film, obviously. She was with some next man.

ZAID. Did she see you?

NEELAM. I sold her a large popcorn.

ZAID. Shit.

NEELAM. She was looking all hot and sophisticated and look at me – like a fucking loser.

ZAID. She's the loser. What did she say?

NEELAM. She was being… nice.

ZAID. Bitch.

NEELAM. She's watching the Japanese film in screen four.

ZAID. She should stick to the Ilford Cineworld.

NEELAM. I wanna die.

ZAID. It's not that bad. Look, let's do lunch, my treat. I'm on break in…

   ZAID *pulls out his phone and gets distracted.*

NEELAM. What's wrong?

ZAID. My play got rejected.

NEELAM. What?

ZAID. My play got rejected for the writing scheme. Just got an email.

NEELAM. Fuck.

ZAID. It's fine, I knew it was shit.

NEELAM. It wasn't shit.

ZAID. Real talk.

NEELAM. It wasn't completely shit.

ZAID. Thanks.

NEELAM. You said real talk. Look, you can write, you know you can write. It's just…

ZAID. What?

NEELAM. It didn't feel like you.

ZAID. What do you mean?

NEELAM. It felt like the play you thought would get you attention, that they would put on.

ZAID. I wanted to write it.

NEELAM. *Closet Boi*?

ZAID. Yeah. *Closet Boi*… How DL men negotiate the world, told through hook-ups. It's a good idea.

NEELAM. Where's the truth?

ZAID. It's just a story. Nobody wants to hear about my boring life.

NEELAM. Draw from it. Be honest, tell the truth.

ZAID. I'm a gay man who works part-time as a cinema usher and whose last dalliance was over two months ago.

NEELAM. Maybe stop calling it a dalliance. Look, you're handsome, entertaining, a great writer, who just needs the right topic.

ZAID. Wish a guy would think so.

NEELAM. You could write about what happened to you when you were fifteen. Explore that.

ZAID. What happened to me?

NEELAM. That guy.

ZAID. Every time you bring this up, you make me wish I never told you. Nothing happened. I was bored and horny and I met a guy.

NEELAM. You were fifteen.

ZAID. Most people lose their virginity at fifteen. It's not a thing.

NEELAM. With other fifteen-year-olds.

ZAID. Yeah, I knew what I was doing.

NEELAM. Really?

ZAID. Yes, I hit on him. Anyway, a good story doesn't need to be true, just reflect a truth, that's what Jeremy said.

NEELAM. And he knows everything. Look, forget it. Me and my big mouth.

ZAID. Check your email.

NEELAM *checks her phone*.

Well?

NEELAM. I got on the scheme, they want to have a chat about the play.

ZAID. YES! Yes. That's big.

NEELAM. It's just a scheme.

ZAID. But a chat as well?

NEELAM. They probably chat to everyone on the course.

ZAID. You don't have to spare my feelings. THIS IS BIG! How many plays have we written and this is the first time anyone has wanted to chat.

NEELAM. Suppose.

ZAID. Tonight we celebrate. Me and you. Theatre!

NEELAM. I thought you said celebrate?

***

Offices at the theatre.

JEREMY. Is this your first play?

NEELAM. I've been on a few different writing programmes, just no interest in any of my others.

JEREMY. Well this has real promise. You have a deep understanding of that community.

NEELAM. Community?

JEREMY. The character was British Pakistani?

NEELAM. Yeah.

JEREMY. It's a voice we definitely need more of on our stages.

NEELAM. Agreed.

JEREMY. Have some thoughts around the stakes, at certain points they could just be higher.

NEELAM. Right. Having sex outside of marriage when you're a Muslim Pakistani girl is already quite high stakes.

JEREMY. Exactly that, but if we could see more of the wider impact of that. It's apparent that you understand all this, but an audience might not.

NEELAM. Suppose it depends on the audience.

JEREMY. True. But clarity is always useful.

NEELAM. Right.

JEREMY. Again these are just suggestions. Take or leave what you like.

Similarly with her parents at the end… the consequences. They stop her from going to university?

NEELAM. No. They stop her from living out at university. They gave her freedom but then she fucks up… sorry. It's about the guilt they put on her. Ultimately I suppose she just needs to stand up to them, but she can't yet. It's the same with mine.

It's a coming-of-age story, how everyone has to break that cord, to some degree.

JEREMY. I got that and it was lovely. But I wonder if the fallout was bigger, more dramatic. I was reading in the paper about an honour killing…

NEELAM. That's not this story.

JEREMY. I wasn't suggesting. I was just saying… Something bigger. That it really builds to something, sheds light into that world. We'd like to see another draft, happy to send you fuller notes or talk at any point.

NEELAM. Right. So you'll pay me to write it?

JEREMY. We don't have the budget for that.

NEELAM. I work in a cinema. Right now. I work in a cinema making minimum wage, I hopped a Tube to make it to this meeting. I have a tonne of student debt for a degree that turns out was pointless and I turn twenty-five next month.

JEREMY. I know it's a struggle. But the powers-that-be are programming next year at the moment and your play would fit really well in that season. There's definitely a big interest. If you made the changes I suggested it would give it a really strong chance.

NEELAM. So you want me to change my play for your white audience and you're not even going to pay me?

***

Call-centre training.

NEELAM. My name is Neelam and I'm calling you today on behalf of 'Save the Dogs'. *Fucking white people and their fucking dogs.*

ZAID. They monitor these.

NEELAM. You gave us a donation in the past, because of your valuable gift we were able to rehome Albert the Yorkshire Terrier. Thank you. Did you know with a regular gift of just five pounds a month we could rehome many more abandoned dogs. *While humans literally die across the world.* Would you be able to help with a regular donation of five pounds?

ZAID. No, sorry, I'm a pensioner and can't afford it.

NEELAM. I completely understand. *Your generation benefited from cheap property prices, higher relative wages and pensions that actually meant something. But still you're a tight-fisted git.* Could you help by donating just two pound a month?

ZAID. Yes.

NEELAM. That's great, you *old codger*, now go and get your debit card – Your turn.

ZAID. Think you have to read out the Direct Debit guarantee.

NEELAM. YOUR TURN!

ZAID. Hi, is that Mrs Smith?

NEELAM. Ms Smith.

ZAID. My name is Zaid.

NEELAM. What kind of a name is that?

ZAID. Ms Smith, I'm calling you on behalf of St Vincent's children's charity.

NEELAM. Are you a Paki?

ZAID. Neelam!

NEELAM. This is shit, Zaid.

ZAID. Neelam, it's thirteen pound an hour and we choose when we work.

NEELAM. Another fucking shit job. Even the cinema is better than this.

ZAID. They're cutting back on hours.

NEELAM. Fuck all of this. Why are we doing it?

ZAID. We'll get time to write.

NEELAM. For pretentious white people like Jeremy. Who don't even get it.

ZAID. He's not that bad.

NEELAM. It's not just him, I sent my play to other theatres.

ZAID. What did they say?

NEELAM. Got my last rejection today.

ZAID. Well then you keep going.

NEELAM. I don't wanna do it any more. I'm tired. I definitely don't want to do this.

ZAID. This job is a means to an end.

NEELAM. I have a fucking degree. I'm gonna bounce.

ZAID. You're just gonna leave?

NEELAM. Yes, we deserve more than this… You coming?

ZAID.

NEELAM. Call me later.

  NEELAM *leaves,* ZAID *puts his hand up.*

ZAID. Sorry, I think I might need another partner for the role-play.

***

Club. High off their faces. An indie classic plays.

NEELAM. Can you feel anything?

ZAID. Yeah. Yeah. Can you?

NEELAM. ███████████

ZAID. Yeah!

   They both uncontrollably laugh.

   I love you. █████████████████████

NEELAM. I love you too.

ZAID. ████████ I love the bones of you.

NEELAM. ███████

ZAID. I LOVE THE BONES OF YOU.

███████

NEELAM. I love the skin of you.

ZAID. The teeth of you.

NEELAM. ███████

ZAID. ███████

NEELAM. ███████

   A moment of intense connection.

   ███████ we're gonna be fine.

ZAID. We're gonna be fucking brilliant.

27

Empty lecture hall.

DEJI. You need to stop talking like that.

NEELAM. Like what, bruv.

DEJI. Point in case. Think I should be the one to speak in our presentation.

NEELAM. My man needs to remember he's from Croydon.

DEJI. Man's, from Purley.

NEELAM. We get it… you went to a private school.

DEJI. 'Listen up, your honour, I don't business, but see brae over there he's innocent.'

NEELAM. Is that supposed to be an impression of me?

DEJI. That's you in court.

NEELAM. We haven't decided our specialism. Maybe I'm going be a solicitor then I won't be in court. Details matter. Probably why I'm on for a distinction and you're not.

DEJI. I'm not far behind. Also heard you tell the tutor you wanted to be a barrister one day.

NEELAM. It's really competitive, especially when you're not from Purley. So we'll see.

DEJI. Well you are good at arguing.

NEELAM. The other thing you got wrong is no *brae* is ever innocent, men are always guilty.

DEJI. Damn who hurt you?

NEELAM. Patriarchy.

DEJI. Deep.

***

Phone.

NEELAM. His name is Deji.

ZAID. Deji? Where's that name from?

***

Empty lecture room.

DEJI. We got eighty!

NEELAM. Not so bad at speaking after all.

DEJI. I'll admit sometimes you can sound eloquent.

NEELAM. Sometimes? If I wasn't mistaken that might be verging on a compliment. You feeling okay, bruv?

DEJI. Could give you other compliments.

NEELAM. Really?

DEJI. But they might not be appropriate.

NEELAM. Why don't you let me be the judge of that.

DEJI. You look like Princess Jasmine.

NEELAM. That was your compliment?

DEJI. Your eyes. You have the most stunning eyes.

    Beat.

NEELAM. Maybe we should get on with our assignment.

***

On the phone: ZAID *waiting in a pub,* NEELAM *in her room.*

NEELAM. He's smart, but chill. Defo the best person on my course.

ZAID. He's Black and not even Muslim, your parents would have a fit.

NEELAM. Thanks, Mum. Nothing's even going on.

ZAID. They gave you enough grief for just moving out.

NEELAM. Called home yesterday and my dad actually said *Salam*. Most I've got out of him in months.

My *poupie* has been trying to get him to see reason.

ZAID. We both know you could have been a lawyer without leaving London.

NEELAM. 'Not my fault Nottingham is the only place to accept me.'

ZAID. You're beginning to believe your own lie.

NEELAM. This was my one chance to escape.

ZAID. Life's boring without you.

NEELAM. You're on a first date.

ZAID. If he ever shows up.

NEELAM. You'll have to come up and stay.

ZAID. Not sure when. Said yes to being supervisor at the cinema.

NEELAM. At least you can quit at the call centre?

ZAID. No. Student finance said they won't fund the Creative Writing BA, because it technically counts as a second degree. Going to have to do the degree part-time. Which means I'm stuck at home forever.

NEELAM. Fucking hell, Zaid. Do you wanna do that?

ZAID. What choice do I have?

NEELAM. There are other things.

ZAID. All the free courses are for under-twenty-fives, and even though my Grindr says different, that's not me any more.

NEELAM. No I meant like, other avenues to pursue.

ZAID. All I want to do is write – It's the one thing that makes sense to me.

NEELAM. Is it worth having to do all the other shit?

ZAID. You should have rewritten that play.

NEELAM. I wasn't going to be a coconut sell-out.

ZAID. You have to play the game.

NEELAM. So you would?

ZAID. No one's asking me.

NEELAM. It will happen for you. Better go, we've been on the phone for three hours!

ZAID. No worries, he's here. Fuck, he looks nothing like his picture.

***

Lecture room.

NEELAM. You've had an Asian girlfriend before.

DEJI. Yeah, for a bit in high school. Before she got scared her parents would find out.

NEELAM. Classic Asian girl.

DEJI. Are you a classic Asian girl?

NEELAM. What do you think?

DEJI. Still trying to work it out.

NEELAM. You ever had a Black girlfriend?

DEJI. No.

NEELAM. Shameful.

DEJI. Hold up, I've dated them. Just never progresses. You?

NEELAM. Never dated a Black girl.

DEJI. Neelam.

NEELAM. Or guy. So you have a fetish for Asian girls?

DEJI. One girl in Year 12 and another at uni.

NEELAM. Two now is it. Sounds like a fetish to me.

DEJI. No. Although if I could find a hot girl who would make me biryani on a regular, might have to put a ring on it.

NEELAM. So you have a biryani fetish?

DEJI. Now you're getting it. Love a girl naked covered in chicken and rice.

NEELAM. That's too far.

DEJI. My best mate from home, Saleem, his mum makes the best Pakistani food.

NEELAM. Does she now? Maybe you should date her.

DEJI. I would, but not sure Saleem or his dad would be happy.

NEELAM. You know I can't cook?

DEJI. I can. I'll teach you.

NEELAM. Right. So what you making me? Egusi?

DEJI. I can't make that. I make a sick jollof though.

NEELAM. Not what I asked for, and I actually prefer Ghanaian to be honest.

DEJI. No, she didn't... let me tell you, once you get a taste for Nigerian jollof nothing else quite hits the spot.

NEELAM. Is that so?

DEJI. Yeah.

Beat

NEELAM. You better give me a taste then.

***

Phone: ZAID *at work,* NEELAM *in a café.*

NEELAM. She posted pictures. Did you see?

ZAID. Yeah. You okay? Can't talk long. I'm not officially on a break.

NEELAM. Yeah, yeah, why wouldn't I be?

Beat.

ZAID. Personally, I think she looked a hot mess.

NEELAM. Do you think?

ZAID. Totally. I thought the icing was meant to be for the cake, not her face.

NEELAM. Stop it. She looked beautiful.

ZAID. Don't get me started on the wedding *lehnga*. She looked like a used tampon.

NEELAM. When have you ever seen a tampon?

ZAID. It's what I imagine a tampon would look like. Everyone rated Rehana in sixth form, but she's basic. Actually look at her. You're much prettier.

NEELAM. She's always been hot.

ZAID. Like Tyra would say, you're high-fashion she's commercial.

NEELAM. It's weird. I just thought that I'd be there. She'd talk loads about her wedding growing up.

ZAID. A basic bitch would.

NEELAM. It's a girl thing, we promised we'd be each other's maids of honour.

ZAID. Look, you don't talk any more. Why would she invite you? Why would you even go?

NEELAM. We have history.

ZAID. History doesn't mean shit. Look what she did to you. You're better off without someone like that.

NEELAM. Suppose.

ZAID. All she's gonna be is some boring housewife. Her biggest achievement in life is going to be this and probably having an ugly kid.

NEELAM. Stop it.

ZAID. What?

NEELAM. Don't want to be basic, but I do eventually want to get married and have kids one day. Don't you?

ZAID.

NEELAM. Sorry, I wasn't thinking.

ZAID. It's fine. And you'll never be basic.

NEELAM. Thanks.

ZAID. Better get back to dialling. They introduced a call rate per hour. Dickheads.

                              ***

Jeremy's office.

ZAID. You don't remember me?

JEREMY. Sorry…

ZAID. I tried to get on the writers' scheme at the theatre three years ago. I didn't.

JEREMY. That was the last scheme I was in charge of.

ZAID. How come?

JEREMY. New Artistic Director. Out with the old, in with the new. Now I only teach creative writing here at the university. Sorry, I can't quite place you? I've met so many young people, becomes impossible after a while.

ZAID. Nice of you to think of me as young. To everyone else on the BA I'm the weird old mature student.

JEREMY. You're not old, I'm old.

ZAID. You don't look it.

    Beat.

JEREMY. *Closet Boi*? Your play? I think.

ZAID. Yeah. God, that's embarrassing.

JEREMY. I didn't read it, but remember you talking about it quite passionately.

ZAID. Glad you didn't. Would never write that now.

JEREMY. Have a drawer stuffed with plays from my youth, dare not open it.

ZAID. That fills me with hope. I saw your last play. Loved it.

JEREMY. You really are doing wonders for my ego.

ZAID. I'm fangirling too hard right? Any other plays coming up?

JEREMY. Nothing imminent, working on the new ones.

ZAID. Look forward to seeing them.

JEREMY. Time to talk about the course, I think.

ZAID. If we have to.

***

Phone.

NEELAM. Jeremy?

ZAID. Yeah, Jeremy.

NEELAM. Old-man Jeremy.

ZAID. Think you mean DILF Jeremy.

NEELAM. No, no, I definitely mean old-man Jeremy.

***

Walking away from the theatre.

ZAID. Nice not to have to sit in the cheap seats for once. Thanks for inviting me.

JEREMY. Thanks for being my plus-one.

ZAID. Would be amazing to have a play on there one day.

JEREMY. That place used to feel like a home away from home.

ZAID. You know everyone. The literary manager loved you.

JEREMY. Still hasn't read a play I sent her six months ago. You should definitely email her though.

ZAID. She wasn't interested in me, but thanks for the introduction.

Beat.

What did you think of it? The play.

JEREMY. Well… The design was nice.

ZAID. The design *was* nice.

JEREMY. And the canapés were great.

They laugh.

I thought you were really enjoying the play.

ZAID. God no.

JEREMY. But you were talking so passionately about it all at the interval.

ZAID. I've had a few now, so the truth comes out.

JEREMY. *In vino veritas.*

ZAID. What?

JEREMY. Latin, 'there is truth in the wine'.

ZAID. You're so hot… I meant to say smart. You're so smart.

JEREMY. Thank you.

Beat.

ZAID. My first-ever press night.

JEREMY. Well, I'll have to invite you to the next one.

ZAID. Really? I'd like that. I'd like that a lot.

***

Phone: NEELAM *walking to meet* DEJI, ZAID *at home.*

NEELAM. Is he allowed to?

ZAID. It's not like I'm some eighteen-year-old.

NEELAM. Still, I've never trusted him.

ZAID. He's actually really sweet.

NEELAM. Just be careful.

****

The quad, walking up to university.

JEREMY. She *was* eating real dogshit.

ZAID. So gross.

JEREMY. Yes, *Pink Flamingos* must have felt like a baptism of fire.

ZAID. You need to make me a list of other films to watch.

JEREMY. Happy to.

ZAID. I enjoyed the film, but waking up with you this morning was definitely the highlight.

JEREMY. You're very cuddly in the morning.

ZAID. So are you. I'll head into the building before you so we're not seen together.

JEREMY. Silly university guidelines.

ZAID. I'm used to keeping things separate. Back to being just student and lecturer.

JEREMY. Yes.

ZAID. One very very horny student.

JEREMY. Still?

ZAID. Meet me in your office in five minutes.

JEREMY. We really shouldn't.

ZAID. No. But there is no way I'll be able to concentrate all day…

JEREMY. Right, well. If it's to aid in your learning.

ZAID. Very much so. See you in five. Professor.

   ZAID *walks off.*

JEREMY. See you in five.

A smiling JEREMY *follows behind.*

***

Phone: NEELAM *walking to meet* DEJI, ZAID *at home.*

ZAID. You're always telling me to live a little. I'm having fun for once.

NEELAM. Can't you have fun with people your own age?

ZAID. I'm the only twenty-eight-year-old on my course, the rest of them are babies. Went out with them last week and never felt so old. Ended up leaving and spent the night at Jeremy's.

NEELAM. What did you tell your parents?

ZAID. I'm working night shifts calling Australia.

NEELAM. Wow, that's elite Asian girling. There must be someone your own age?

ZAID. I'm interested in Jeremy, it has real potential – we hang out all the time.

NEELAM. Just couldn't imagine having sex with any of my lecturers.

ZAID. That's because you're loved-up.

NEELAM. Shut up.

ZAID. Have you said it?

NEELAM. He did.

ZAID. Really… Did you say it back?

NEELAM. Yeah. And I don't need a lecture about how it's not going to work long term. I'm just living in the moment.

ZAID. I wasn't. Happy for you. You deserve someone nice.

NEELAM. Thanks, Zaid.

ZAID. Wonder what's worse for our parents, a gay son or daughter with a Black boyfriend?

***

Jeremy's flat. Classical musical playing in the background.

JEREMY. Told you I could handle my spice.

ZAID. I'll know better than to underestimate you.

JEREMY. Thank you for coming over and cooking for me. Next time it'll be my turn.

ZAID. As long as I'm in charge of the music.

JEREMY. This not doing it for you?

ZAID. Not really. Need to introduce you to something from this decade.

JEREMY. Deal.

ZAID. Read the first draft you sent me.

JEREMY. That was quick.

ZAID. Flattered that you'd even ask. Wish my first drafts would come out as fully formed.

JEREMY. Your first drafts show promise, as I keep telling you. You need to have more confidence.

ZAID. Thanks. I do have a big note, but just ignore it if you want.

JEREMY. Hit me with it.

ZAID. You probably don't need the first scene.

JEREMY. The whole scene?

ZAID. Actually, all of the bit before they get married.

JEREMY. That's a big change.

ZAID. Like you say, get straight into the action.

JEREMY. Can't argue with my own words. Thanks.

ZAID. Any time. Was the play based on your own life?

JEREMY. Elements...

ZAID. So, you were married?

JEREMY. Civil partnership. Bit of a mistake in hindsight. We were in such a rush to get this new-found freedom, to be like the straights. We didn't really question if it was right for us. But unlike the play we never adopted. We were wise enough to know that would have been a disaster.

ZAID. You don't ever want kids?

JEREMY. No.

ZAID. Me neither. How long were you together?

JEREMY. Over a decade.

ZAID. Wow. Keep in touch?

JEREMY. God no, I'm not a lesbian. Once that door's closed, it's closed.

ZAID. Yeah, I've never got this 'keep in touch with my ex' thing.

JEREMY. Sometimes it's just the healthier option.

ZAID. Yeah. Do you think you ever would again?

JEREMY. Marriage? No. I'm too old for all that.

ZAID. You need to stop with the 'old' stuff.

JEREMY. Well then maybe too wise to buy into all that heteronormative nonsense again. Don't want to feel beholden to anyone and vice versa, I want every day to have that spark of the beginning. Life's too short.

***

Neelam's university accommodation. NEELAM *is getting ready, there is a knock at the door.*

NEELAM. For fuck's sake, Deji. On the one day I could have done with you adhering to Black-man time.

    NEELAM *opens the door, it's* ZAID.

ZAID. Surprise. HAPPY BIRTHDAY!

NEELAM. You're not supposed be here till tomorrow.

ZAID. Today is the actual day of your birthday… Plus, just needed to get out of London. Everything is so fucked.

NEELAM. Right, but…

ZAID. And I thought you wouldn't mind.

NEELAM. Of course not. Is everything okay?

ZAID. No.

NEELAM. What's going on then?

ZAID. Home is depressing as always. My brother just won't move out and his wife is pregnant. A screaming baby in that small house.

NEELAM. Is that it?

ZAID. And I think me and Jeremy are over. He said he wants to be open.

NEELAM. What does that mean?

ZAID. That we just fuck? I don't know.

NEELAM. I'm sorry.

ZAID. Why can't I just meet someone and it be uncomplicated?

NEELAM. Know you might not want to hear this right now, but maybe it's a good thing.

ZAID. That I'm single, stuck at home and can't fucking get a break.

NEELAM. Real talk. Like the whole relationship with Jeremy was just not healthy.

ZAID. If you're going to start again with him being my tutor.

NEELAM. It's an abuse of his position. He should know better.

ZAID. It's a creative writing degree and I'm fully grown. Like give it some context.

NEELAM. Still. Maybe you're just repeating the patterns of your past?

ZAID. What do you mean by that?

NEELAM. Just, maybe repeating unhealthy dynamics.

ZAID. Look, I just need cheering up with my best mate, I didn't ask for real talk and definitely didn't ask for psychoanalysing.

NEELAM. If we can't tell each other the truth, then?

ZAID. I know, just not now. Please. Not seen you in ages and right now I've got some mandy in my pocket and I just want us to get high.

NEELAM. I can't. I'm supposed to be seeing Deji.

ZAID. Right.

NEELAM. He booked a restaurant for my birthday. Thought that was him at the door.

ZAID. Sorry, should have clocked you would've had plans. My bad.

NEELAM. No, you can come whenever. You know that.

ZAID. What time are you done?

NEELAM. No, don't be stupid. Come with innit?

ZAID. Nah, I couldn't do that.

NEELAM. Of course you can. Deji will be chill.

ZAID. Really?

NEELAM. Yes really. About time you both met.

ZAID. Okay.

NEELAM. You gonna wear that?

***

Bar after dinner – ZAID, NEELAM, DEJI.

ZAID. She just walked out. Right in the middle of the training, you should have seen the look on the woman's face who was running the thing.

NEELAM. Oh, mate, she was too annoying.

DEJI. You should see her in lectures, this one time…

ZAID. EMMA! Was her name Emma?

NEELAM. No. Like some kind of flower vibe.

ZAID. Daisy? LILLY!

NEELAM. LILLY!

ZAID/NEELAM. 'PILLY LILLY.'

They laugh, DEJI *politely.*

DEJI. I don't get it.

NEELAM. She looked like she was on something the whole
time.

ZAID. Neelam, don't, turns out she had Graves' disease.

DEJI. That's not funny.

NEELAM. You're right. Sorry.

ZAID. I mean she was still a pain in the ass.

NEELAM. That call centre was the low point that led to
studying law.

DEJI. Really?

ZAID. Some of us are stupid enough to still work there.

NEELAM. Because you're going to be a writer. It'll be worth it
in the end.

ZAID. But not for you?

NEELAM. Not any more.

ZAID. You know Neelam is an amazing writer.

DEJI. This is news to me.

NEELAM. It's not true.

ZAID. It is.

NEELAM. Why are you bringing this up, Zaid? It's my birthday.

ZAID. And we're celebrating you. She could have had a play on and everything.

DEJI. That's impressive.

ZAID. At like one of the most prestigious theatres in London. Surprised she didn't tell you.

DEJI. My girl, full of hidden talents.

NEELAM. Zaid is grossly over-exaggerating.

ZAID. 'He Who Shall Not Be Named' told me they were really interested.

NEELAM. You spoke about me and the play to Jeremy.

ZAID. It just came up. Anyway, thought you didn't care?

NEELAM. I don't. Was never going to write the play they wanted, so it was never gonna happen.

ZAID. You never even tried.

NEELAM. Because I didn't want to, Zaid. Do you know how much happier I am now?

ZAID. Really?

NEELAM. I'm not waiting around for the day I'll make it.

ZAID. By doing a law conversion course?

NEELAM. I'm really fucking good at it and I'll get paid. Plus, if I didn't come here I would never have met Deji.

NEELAM *kisses* DEJI. *ZAID is the third wheel.*

ZAID. I'll shut up then. So, Deji, what failed ambition led you to a law conversion course?

NEELAM. Zaid!

DEJI. I always wanted to be a lawyer.

ZAID. Really?

DEJI. Yeah.

ZAID. So even like when you were a kid when people asked you what you wanted to be, you'd say lawyer?

DEJI. No. When I was a kid I wanted to be Batman. But then we all grow up.

NEELAM. Think you'd look good as Batman.

DEJI. Thanks, babe.

ZAID. I wanted to be Wonder Woman.

NEELAM. You'd look good as Wonder Woman too.

ZAID. I would, wouldn't I.

DEJI. Shall I get the bill then?

NEELAM (*to* DEJI). You paid for dinner.

ZAID. I'll get the next round when we move on to Hockley. That's where all the gay bars are, right? And someone brought mandy.

    ZAID *flashes a baggy.*

DEJI. That's not my vibe.

NEELAM. Deji doesn't do drugs.

ZAID. It's not drugs, it's MDMA.

NEELAM. Zaid.

DEJI. If you both want to go ahead.

NEELAM. I don't really want to either. I've kinda stopped.

ZAID. This is news.

NEELAM. Yes. Need a clear head, we've got exams next week.

ZAID. Right. Just me then.

    Beat.

    Joking.

***

Lecture hall. DEJI headphones in. NEELAM taps him on the shoulder. He pulls off his headphones.

NEELAM. What you listening to?

DEJI. Classical music.

NEELAM. Classical music!

DEJI. What's wrong with that? Meant to help you study.

NEELAM. Okay then.

Beat.

Haven't seen you since my birthday.

DEJI. Just been revising.

NEELAM. Revising.

DEJI. Yeah.

NEELAM. We're on the same course.

DEJI. Thought some independent study might do me good.

NEELAM. I apologised, Zaid just showed up. I didn't know what to do, he was going through some shit.

DEJI. A tiff with his boyfriend, sorry, meant non-monogamous partner.

NEELAM. Do you have an issue with him being gay?

DEJI. What?

NEELAM. You acted off the whole night

DEJI. Why would you even say that? Because I'm a Black man?

NEELAM. Because you're a man.

DEJI. Really? Sure it's not more? All those off-key comments about Black-man time and the rest of that shit, suddenly make sense.

NEELAM. It's a joke. I'll stop if it bothers you that much.

DEJI. It does.

NEELAM. Maybe you want to stop calling me Princess
    Jasmine all the time then.

DEJI. I will.

Beat.

NEELAM. What's really going on?

DEJI. Just don't appreciate being the third wheel on a date with
    my own girlfriend.

NEELAM. So just come out and say that. Instead of all this shit.

DEJI. What's the point?

NEELAM. Because that's what couples do.

DEJI. And we're a couple?

NEELAM. Are we not?

DEJI. What happens when we go home for the summer? We
    gonna see each other? In a year's time when we graduate?
    Will that be it? You go back to your world and I'll go back to
    mine and none of this ever happened?

NEELAM. No.

DEJI. So you would tell your parents about me? Your Black
    boyfriend.

NEELAM. Would you tell yours about me, your bit of rough?

DEJI. Yeah. Yeah I would.

NEELAM. Then so would I. I love you.

DEJI. I love you more.

***

Club. High off their faces. An indie classic plays.

NEELAM. ███████████████

ZAID. ███████████

NEELAM. ▮

ZAID. ▮

They both uncontrollably laugh.

I love you. ▮

NEELAM. I love you ▮

ZAID. ▮ the bones of you.

NEELAM. ▮

ZAID. I LOVE THE BONES OF YOU.

▮

NEELAM. ▮ skin ▮

ZAID. ▮ teeth ▮

NEELAM. ▮

ZAID. ▮

NEELAM. ▮

A moment of intense connection.

▮ we're gonna be fine.

ZAID. We're gonna be fucking brilliant.

32

Deji and Neelam's flat.

ZAID. London, baby.

NEELAM. Zone five, baby.

ZAID. Well Edgware is closer to me than Nottingham so I'm happy.

NEELAM. As long as you're happy.

ZAID. Come on, admit that you're excited to be back?

NEELAM. Being back makes it more real, how fucked everything is with my family.

ZAID. Right, I'm sorry. But at least we get to relive our glory days.

NEELAM. Maybe one of the pluses of Deji getting a pupillage in London is that I'll get to see more of you.

ZAID. Yes! And you'll get yours the next time you apply. Especially now you've got that job doing the thing at the thing.

NEELAM. Law centre specialising in immigration.

ZAID. That's what I said.

NEELAM. Yeah next time the posh wankers won't be able to say no.

ZAID. Definitely. I'm so excited. This is like when the Spice Girls announced the reunion tour.

NEELAM. Yes, yes, it's exactly like that.

***

Jeremy's flat.

ZAID. What time is he going to be here?

JEREMY. I'll text and ask him.

> JEREMY *pulls out his phone.*

ZAID. No, don't. Actually, go on then.

JEREMY *sends a message.*

JEREMY. You're okay?

ZAID. Yeah.

JEREMY. You sure.

ZAID. Yeah, just nervous.

JEREMY. This is meant to be fun.

ZAID. Maybe we should've just gone to dinner. I'm joking.

JEREMY. Relax.

ZAID. He's never seen me.

JEREMY. He's seen pictures.

ZAID. Different when you meet someone in person. He's definitely into Asian guys?

JEREMY. He's Asian himself.

ZAID. I know, but sometimes other Asians aren't. Do you hook up with a lot of Asian guys? Actually, don't. We don't tell each other. I like that.

JEREMY. Think that was your rule. Happy to share if you want me to?

ZAID. No don't

Beat.

JEREMY. I'm going to cancel.

JEREMY *goes to his phone.*

ZAID. What? No, you don't have to.

JEREMY. Done.

JEREMY *puts his phone away.*

ZAID. Sorry.

JEREMY. Why are you apologising?

ZAID. Thought I wanted to try it. But I don't know…

JEREMY. This was your idea, but if it's causing you anxiety.

ZAID. In my head it felt hot. Just don't know how I'd react seeing you with someone else. What if it changed things?

JEREMY. I love you, Zaid, it'd take a lot for something to change that for me.

ZAID. I love you too.

They kiss.

***

Deji and Neelam's flat.

DEJI. Babe, they didn't have any whole-nut. Edgware is the ghetto.

NEELAM *walks in.*

NEELAM. I finally got my period.

DEJI. That's a good thing, right?

NEELAM. I think so.

Beat.

DEJI. Did you want to be pregnant?

NEELAM. You know people our age have kids. We're not in our twenties any more.

DEJI. I know.

NEELAM. Thirty-two. I'm not far off being a geriatric mum.

DEJI. You wanted it to be a baby?

NEELAM. When I thought I could be, part of me was happy. The decision was made.

DEJI. And the other part?

NEELAM. What about becoming a barrister? Applying for the pupillage.

DEJI. That's important.

NEELAM. Most of the girls I went to school with are posting pictures of their second or third. Fiona at work has had rounds of IVF and nothing.

DEJI. Maybe we should then?

NEELAM. Also couldn't help thinking, what about my parents...

DEJI. Right.

NEELAM. Know it's stupid, I'm a grown woman and I haven't spoken to them since I told them we got together so what does it matter? But if I have a kid I want my family to be part of that as well.

DEJI. They're the ones who chose not to have you in their lives.

NEELAM. You know my *poupie* thinks if we had a *nikah* it would help.

DEJI. But I need to be Muslim in order for us to have an Islamic wedding. And I've already said I'm not converting.

NEELAM. You could just pretend. Get my parents to reconcile to the idea of me and you.

DEJI. Right. So, me pretending to be Muslim means me being Black isn't so bad?

NEELAM. I know it sounds fucked up.

DEJI. Yeah it does

NEELAM. They're the only family I've got.

DEJI. And what happens when we do have a kid and it comes out as dark-skinned as his dad? How is your family going to react to that?

NEELAM. Probably the same as your family will.

DEJI. What do you mean by that?

NEELAM. I'm no way posh enough for your mum, to be with her prince of a son. And she's more than happy to remind me every time she sees me.

DEJI. That's all in your head.

NEELAM. 'My children are my investment, wouldn't want anything lowering the stock.'

DEJI. My parents sacrificed a lot for me. Worked two jobs each so I could go to a better school.

NEELAM. And mine didn't sacrifice for me?

DEJI. I'm just saying you're taking her words out of context.

NEELAM. What other context is there? The constant digs about the way I grew up, how I talk. Like she's the fucking queen. My parents did the best they could.

DEJI. My parents might be a lot of things, but they're not a bunch of small-minded racists. At least they can stand to be in the same room as you.

NEELAM. Tell them not to do me any favours. Because if you can't even understand what I'm asking you, well then you should fuck off back to them.

DEJI. And you mean that?

NEELAM. Yeah.

DEJI. Right, I'll do that then.

    DEJI *walks off*.

***

Club.

NEELAM. Where have you been?

ZAID. Was talking to some guy.

NEELAM. You mean you were tonguing him?

ZAID. No. He just gave me a blowjob.

NEELAM. Gays. And your open relationships.

ZAID. Stop being so heterosexual.

NEELAM. Well, stop neglecting me.

ZAID. When did you become so needy?

NEELAM. I've always been needy, you were just needier.

ZAID. *In vino veritas.*

NEELAM. You're not with Jeremy now, talk normal. So good to hear some indie music. Be in an actual club.

ZAID. When was the last time you did this?

NEELAM. Too long.

ZAID. You and Deji never go out out?

NEELAM. He'd never come to an indie night.

ZAID. Not his vibe?

Indie anthem #2 plays.

NEELAM. Fuck yes!!

She pulls ZAID *to dance.*

ZAID. Not this song. It's so tired now.

NEELAM. What?

ZAID. It's just become the preserve of basic bitches. It's so played out they even know it in Ilford now.

NEELAM. Don't do that.

ZAID. Do what?

NEELAM. That, 'I'm too cool for this' shit. You love this song. We've always loved this song.

ZAID. Neelam, it's really not that deep.

NEELAM. Yes, Zaid. Yes it is. I came out tonight with my best mate and I've barely seen you all night. And now you're being a fucking giant prick!!

Silence.

ZAID. Are you okay?

NEELAM. Sorry. Sorry, I didn't mean that.

ZAID. What's going on, Neelam?

NEELAM. Deji left to stay at his parents for a bit.

ZAID. What? Why?

NEELAM. Don't even know where to start. Families, always the fucking families.

ZAID *hugs* NEELAM.

ZAID. Why didn't you tell me earlier?

NEELAM. Didn't want to think about it for a bit.

ZAID. I'm sorry.

NEELAM. I don't know, Zaid. I don't know any more. I love him. But maybe that's not enough. And if we break up, what has this all been for?

ZAID. You're not going to break up.

NEELAM. I'm not so sure.

ZAID. He'd be a fucking idiot. He's lucky to have you. Anyone would be.

NEELAM. Thanks, Zaid.

ZAID. Let's dance.

NEELAM. Thought the song was tired?

ZAID. You were right, I'm a dick. Come on. Let's fucking dance.

***

Café, Croydon.

ZAID. Never been to Croydon before.

DEJI. It's Purley.

ZAID. That not the same thing?

DEJI. No.

ZAID. Right.

DEJI. You said you wanted to talk.

ZAID. Neelam told me about what's going on.

DEJI. Did she tell you to speak to me?

ZAID. No. And she'd probably kill me if she knew I was. But here I am.

DEJI. Maybe you shouldn't get involved.

ZAID. She's miserable.

DEJI. Right. Not the impression I got, she was out with you the other night, it was all over her Insta.

ZAID. And she was the least fun she's ever been.

DEJI. I've not been sleeping, can't eat, can't work. Feel like I'm missing a limb.

ZAID. She's really cut up too, you know that?

DEJI. She's not been acting like it. When I left didn't even look at me. Head down, writing.

ZAID. She was writing?

DEJI. Yeah. She writes a lot.

ZAID. Right. All I know is that I've never seen her like this before, the way she is with you. She really loves you.

DEJI. I love her too.

ZAID. So, what the fuck are you both doing?

DEJI. But there's a reality to this.

ZAID. Don't let your families fuck this up for you.

DEJI. What can I do? I'll always be the guy keeping her from her family, it's already starting to poison us.

ZAID. So, don't. Don't be that guy.

DEJI. And what? Pretend to be Muslim, so her family can be racist to my face. Do you know how mad that plan is?

ZAID. I don't think Neelam's family are going to ever be outrightly racist towards you. They're not like that.

DEJI. Outrightly? It's fine if it's under the surface?

ZAID. Look, I don't want to minimise what you're facing. But think about everything Neelam's done for you. She knew what would happen when she told her parents. Knew what it meant.

She was so brave, something I've never been with my own parents about myself. And she did it for you, because she loves you so much.

You've got no reason to listen to me because I'm her mate. But if you try to build a bridge with her family, yeah it might not work, but then at least you'll be the guy who tried to reconcile her with her parents rather than the one who was the barrier. You'll be the good guy.

DEJI. I'm not the barrier, they are. It shouldn't be down to me to build a bridge. And what about my parents? Do they matter? They're not going to be happy with me pretending to be a Muslim.

ZAID. Don't tell them. Simple. Welcome to being Asian.

DEJI. But I'm not, I'm not Asian.

***

Mosque side room.

NEELAM. And my family aren't coming, are they?

ZAID. Did they know which mosque?

NEELAM. Yes.

ZAID. What did your *poupie* say?

NEELAM. She did her best, spoke to them loads. Couldn't guarantee that they would turn up.

ZAID. It doesn't look like they are.

NEELAM. Deji's gonna hate me.

ZAID. No, he won't.

NEELAM. I'm the one forcing him to have an Islamic wedding.

ZAID. He's a big boy and he loves you.

NEELAM. What's the point, if my parents are not even here?

ZAID. That's the only reason you're doing this? For your parents. You don't want this?

NEELAM. I do, I do. I want to get married and want the Muslim bit too.

ZAID. Well then you're doing the right thing.

NEELAM. This isn't how I imagined my wedding, in the side room of a mosque, without my family.

ZAID. I'm here for you as the Man of Honour.

NEELAM. I would have gone with the Best Maid.

ZAID. Jeremy said the same, but I think it makes me sound like I work in a hotel.

NEELAM. Sorry I couldn't invite him, just numbers and stuff.

ZAID. It's cool.

NEELAM. Got the whole Nigerian wedding with Deji and his family as well, and then I'll do a proper celebration at some other point, have more mates there.

ZAID. Chill.

NEELAM. When we go in there, I'm going to need you to be my witness, sign the document. Have you by my side 'cause my dad's not here.

ZAID. Of course. I'd be honoured.

Enter DEJI.

NEELAM. You can't be in here.

DEJI. I know, I know. But I don't have any reception in the other room so I couldn't text. Your mum and dad are here.

NEELAM. They came?

DEJI. Yeah. I just shook his hand, your dad.

NEELAM. Really?

DEJI. Really.

NEELAM. They fucking came. They fucking came. I know how hard this is for you, and I'm sorry I asked you to do something you feel uncomfortable with, but really I can't thank you enough.

DEJI. I did this because I love you.

DEJI *and* NEELAM *kiss*.

NEELAM. I love you too. Now piss off so we can have a *nikah*.

DEJI. Okay. Also... You look fit.

NEELAM. GO!

DEJI *leaves*.

ZAID. They came.

NEELAM. Can't believe it. My parents are here.

ZAID. I'm so happy for you, and you get your dad to be with you.

NEELAM. Yeah, I won't need you as my witness then.

ZAID. Saves me a job.

NEELAM. Actually could you grab my dad? I should probably get him to come in here so I can walk in with him.

ZAID. Sure.

ZAID *walks out*.

                              ***

JEREMY *looking at pictures on* ZAID'*s phone*.

ZAID. She looked beautiful.

JEREMY. She did, a very attractive couple.

ZAID. Weird that she's married. She's doing proper grown-up things. And, well, me...

JEREMY. You're a grown-up too.

ZAID. Doesn't always feel like it.

JEREMY. Time works differently for queers. Those markers of adulthood were designed for them, so it's easier. We need to make our own makers. Maybe we could get a dog?

ZAID. You serious? Neelam would rip me a new one.

JEREMY. Who's this other couple here?

ZAID. That's Deji's friend Saleem I think and his wife.

JEREMY. Thought there wasn't room for partners.

ZAID. Some people did bring them and some people didn't.

JEREMY. And you were one of the ones that didn't?

ZAID. It was numbers.

JEREMY. Right, and that was it?

ZAID. Maybe it would have been awkward.

JEREMY. For you to have your partner there?

ZAID. I suppose.

JEREMY. It worries me, the ease with which you compartmentalise. I'm in a neat little box here and your family over there. You know everyone in my life, I've barely seen a picture of your mother or father

ZAID. What choice do I have?

JEREMY. You do, you choose how you live. How do you know how your family would react if you don't give them the chance? You're not the only gay Pakistani.

ZAID. We've talked about this. I'm not like the posh Pakistanis you know.

JEREMY. What's that got to do with anything? You still have agency, to live life on your terms. That's what being a grown-up is really about.

***

Bedroom – DEJI *getting dressed.*

NEELAM. We need to leave.

DEJI. Had to re-iron my shirt.

NEELAM. Don't ask me next time.

DEJI. We'll make it on time. And my shirt will be extra crisp.

NEELAM. Why am I stressed? It's your work thing, I'm always on time.

DEJI. Your dad text. Wants me to go to the mosque with him. Hoping it's a one-off and he doesn't expect me there every Friday.

NEELAM. He's probably just excited, he'll lose interest.

DEJI. Being a pretend Muslim is harder than it looks.

NEELAM. I can get Zaid to go with you so you've got a buddy.

DEJI. When was the last time he stepped in a mosque?

NEELAM. It's like riding a bicycle, you never forget. Thank you. For making the effort and going along with this.

DEJI. Talking about effort, my mum wants you to wear an *iro* to my cousin's wedding next week.

NEELAM. I'm gonna look like a culturally appropriating idiot.

DEJI. And the *gele*.

NEELAM. Full headwear?

DEJI. It's about making the effort.

NEELAM. Fine.

DEJI. And expect to be quizzed by my mum and aunties about when we're having a baby.

NEELAM. Good enough to have kids with now? What a turnaround.

DEJI. She's just tired of waiting, so anyone will do.

They laugh.

NEELAM. Thanks. Think that's why my parents have come around to this as well. Once you're past thirty you're expired goods, so just marry, and have kids with the first one that will. My mum's been asking when too.

DEJI. Maybe we should tell them we're trying?

NEELAM. Are you mad? That's just going to make it too stressful. You ready?

DEJI. Nearly there.

NEELAM. Do you remember I talked about my old friend Rehana?

DEJI. Not really.

NEELAM. We were inseparable at primary school till sixth form. She heard I got married. Wants to meet for coffee.

DEJI. You going to?

NEELAM. I don't know, we stopped speaking and Zaid hates her.

DEJI. I wouldn't trust Zaid's judgement on anyone.

NEELAM. He's my best mate.

DEJI. You know you're not kids in the playground any more. Things change, people change, she must have reached out for a reason.

NEELAM. Yeah, maybe I'll message her. Nice to be back in the fold. My parents were even boasting about you being a barrister.

DEJI. Only just started the pupillage.

NEELAM. That's not going to stop them from boasting.

DEJI. They'll be boasting about their daughter being one too soon enough.

NEELAM. Yeah, after we've started our family.

DEJI. *Inshallah*.

NEELAM. Oi, get you.

DEJI. Everyone knows *inshallah*. Come on, I'm done.

NEELAM. Come on then, princess.

    NEELAM *gets out her phone*.

    Zaid, his ears really must have been burning… Fuck.

DEJI. Is everything okay?

NEELAM. He's at the hospital, his dad's just had a heart attack.

              ***

Hospital café.

ZAID. No one was at home. God knows how long he was like
    that at the bottom of the stairs.

NEELAM. Who found him?

ZAID. My mum. She called for the ambulance. We thought he
    was gonna be okay.

NEELAM. Then he had a stroke?

ZAID. Yeah.

NEELAM. How is he now?

ZAID. Murmurs a bit.

NEELAM. What have the doctors said?

ZAID. The stats around this stuff aren't good.

NEELAM. I'm sorry, Zaid.

ZAID. Seeing him like this, he was always such a strong man,
    played hockey for Pakistan in his youth.

NEELAM. I remember the picture you showed me.

ZAID. And now look.

NEELAM. How's your mum?

ZAID. A mess. We all are.

Beat.

Keep thinking, if he dies he'll have died not knowing the real me.

NEELAM. He does know the real you.

ZAID. He doesn't know that I'm gay.

NEELAM. That doesn't mean he doesn't know the real you. You're more than just being gay. You know that?

ZAID. But it's a big part of me. A big part of me that I'm hiding. That he'll now never know. I want to tell him, and the rest of my family.

NEELAM. Right. And now is the best time to do this?

ZAID. Don't know how much time he's got.

NEELAM. I don't think you should.

ZAID. I've thought about it a lot.

NEELAM. I think this is a bad idea. A really bad idea.

ZAID. You were brave enough to tell your family about Deji and look how it's all worked out now.

NEELAM. My situation was different.

ZAID. I get it, It's worse to be gay…

NEELAM. No. I had Deji. You'll be doing this alone.

ZAID. I've got Jeremy.

NEELAM. You know it's not the same, Deji was committed to me.

ZAID. Jeremy and I have been together for years.

NEELAM. Is he going to pick up the pieces? Deal with the fallout?

ZAID. He said he thinks it's a good idea. If it's something I need to do.

NEELAM. Of course he would. Because he doesn't have a clue. He's a posh white man, and you're not.

ZAID. You've never liked him.

NEELAM. That's not true. I'm thinking of you. You still live at home, Zaid. Have you thought about that? What it would be like?

ZAID. I could move out.

NEELAM. With what money? And what about your mum? She's going through enough already and you want her to deal with this too?

ZAID. Just want to be honest. Don't want him to die without knowing the real me. Tired of always hiding, always compartmentalising.

NEELAM. You're not in the right place to make this decision. This is me being real with you.

ZAID. I really thought you'd get it.

NEELAM. It's because I love you that I'm saying don't do it.

***

Outside the hospital.

ZAID *on the phone.*

JEREMY. Zaid.

ZAID. Hi.

JEREMY. It's late. You okay?

ZAID. I'm not sure. He died.

JEREMY. I'm so sorry.

ZAID. Just now. I tried calling Neelam, no answer, she must be asleep.

JEREMY. You at the hospital.

ZAID. In the car park. I couldn't stay in there.

Silence.

JEREMY. Alright, I'm coming.

ZAID. No, don't. My family are here.

JEREMY. I don't care.

ZAID. What will I say?

JEREMY. Just tell them I'm a friend.

Beat.

Zaid?

ZAID. Okay. Okay, thank you.

***

Jeremy's flat. ZAID *on his laptop.*

JEREMY. You promise me you won't just sit in the flat all day?

ZAID. Promise.

JEREMY. Make sure you go out? Maybe see what Neelam's up to?

ZAID. Last I heard from her was a week ago.

JEREMY. You could message her?

ZAID. I shouldn't have to. I've got loads of work to be doing anyway.

JEREMY. You can't just be working all the time.

ZAID. I'm fine.

JEREMY. It's okay not to be too

ZAID. I know, I know. It's useful, the distraction of writing.

JEREMY. I could call in sick?

ZAID. You don't need to do that. You've done enough already just letting me stay here.

JEREMY. It's actually been lovely having you here.

ZAID. Would have gone crazy staying at home. Relentless how many people still keep showing up to pay their respects and it's been months.

JEREMY. Must be nice for your mum, having people around. Know mine found it hard when that all stopped.

ZAID. Yeah I suppose.

JEREMY. Come meet me for dinner then? After work?

ZAID. Happy just to order in.

JEREMY. I could actually do with the cheering up. Another polite rejection for the play.

ZAID. They're idiots.

JEREMY. I don't know.

ZAID. They are. It's a brilliant play. Let's do dinner then, you're right, I need to get out.

***

Deji and Neelam's flat. NEELAM *on the phone,* DEJI *watches on.*

NEELAM. Thanks, Mommy, I will. I'll take it easy. Okay bye.

She hands the phone back to DEJI.

DEJI. Sorry my mum insisted that she speak to you.

NEELAM. This is why I told you not to tell anyone.

DEJI. I was excited.

NEELAM. There's a reason you're supposed to wait. I wasn't even eight weeks.

DEJI. You're right. I'm really sorry. Are you okay?

NEELAM. She was actually sweet. Said the same happened to her a couple of times before she had your brother.

DEJI. I didn't know that.

NEELAM. Why would you? My own mum wasn't much use. Felt like she was blaming me.

DEJI. I'm sure she wouldn't have meant it like that.

NEELAM. Told me I should have rested more.

Beat.

Do you think I was doing too much?

DEJI. I don't think so.

NEELAM. I couldn't just lie in bed the whole time.

DEJI. This just happens.

NEELAM. What if it happens again?

DEJI. You're overthinking.

NEELAM. Took it for granted that when I was ready to have a baby that it would just be simple but what if it's not?

DEJI. Then we cross that bridge together, if we come to it.

***

Jeremy's flat.

NEELAM. Jeremy's flat! Can I look through his cupboards?

ZAID. No!

NEELAM. He's got good taste, it can go either way with rich people.

ZAID. Just happy to have anywhere to escape to. The amount of relatives that have visited and the thousands of questions about why I'm not married.

NEELAM. Sounds intense

ZAID. Yep. Lucky to have Jeremy.

NEELAM. Yeah, he's really come through.

How are you holding up?

ZAID. Alright. Life as a married woman still good?

NEELAM. Yeah. The family can still say some off-key things, and not sure my mum will ever get his name right, she really loves him though.

ZAID. That's good. And they still think he's Muslim?

NEELAM. He went to the mosque a couple of times and now they don't really bring it up.

ZAID. Great. And how is Deji?

NEELAM. Sends his love. Barely see him, the workload has been intense, I'm having to pick up the slack.

ZAID. Doesn't sound fun.

NEELAM. He'd do the same for me and it'll be worth it in the end.

ZAID. What about your plans to become a barrister?

NEELAM. It's about the right timing.

ZAID. As long as that's all that it is.

Beat.

So, you've been busy?

NEELAM. I've had stuff going on.

ZAID. Like what?

NEELAM. I don't want to burden you with that.

ZAID. No go on?

NEELAM. Well, I… Just tired. Thought Pakistanis had loads of family functions, you should try being Nigerian.

ZAID. So that's it? That's why I've not seen more of you?

NEELAM. Yeah.

ZAID. I assumed you thought my dad dying was contagious.

NEELAM. Zaid.

ZAID. Bad joke.

NEELAM. Wasn't sure if you wanted to be left alone.

ZAID. You should have asked me what I needed.

NEELAM. You went a bit silent… But I was here as soon as I could, when you text.

ZAID. I shouldn't have had to.

NEELAM. Sorry.

Beat.

ZAID. It's fine. I've had loads of uni work, it's been relentless.

NEELAM. You told them everything?

ZAID. They said I could defer but I'm so close to finishing, just want to get it done.

NEELAM. But you need time.

ZAID. To think about it more than I already am? Whenever I'm out, keep having this urge to go up to strangers and just tell them. Randomly. My dad died of a stroke. Like, how would they react? What would they say? Must look normal to them, but my insides are irrevocably changed. And nobody out there has a clue.

NEELAM. I'm sorry, Zaid.

ZAID. When I dropped out of uni, my mum was livid. Dad came up to me and gave me a big hug, said he'd told her not to push me into that course. He read some of my writing and said that I had the heart of a poet, not a computer scientist.

NEELAM. Remember you saying

ZAID. If I ever do make it as a writer he'll never see that.

NEELAM. When you do.

ZAID. There's so much about me he'll never see or know. So much I regret not telling him. His sensitive little boy.

***

ZAID *reading a text out loud to* JEREMY.

ZAID. Forgive me for not doing this face to face. I wanted to send this in writing because words are my thing. I don't always know what I think or feel on the spot, the blankness of a page helps me to spill it out, to filter the thoughts. To compose myself.

I'm gay. I'm tired of revealing only the bits of me that I think people might love. So this is me. I'm still the same Zaid and I'm still your son and I still love you. I hope you do too.

JEREMY. I think it's beautiful.

ZAID. Real talk?

JEREMY. Sorry?

ZAID. Me and Neelam would… Never mind.

JEREMY. Maybe you want to send it to Neelam first? Get the cultural angle?

Beat.

ZAID. No.

ZAID *presses send.* JEREMY *goes and hugs him.*

***

Club. High off their faces. An indie classic plays.

NEELAM. ██████████████████

ZAID. ███████████████

NEELAM. ████████████

ZAID. ███████

████████████████████████

I love you. █████████████████

NEELAM. I love you █████

ZAID. █████████████ bones █████

NEELAM. ██████

ZAID. ███████████████████

████

NEELAM. 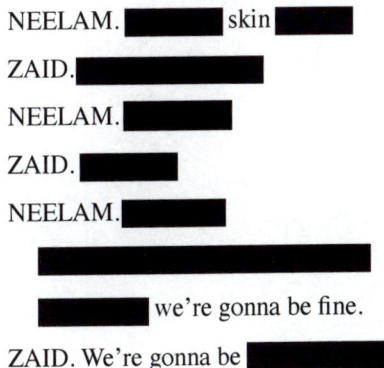 skin ▮

ZAID. ▮

NEELAM. ▮

ZAID. ▮

NEELAM. ▮

▮

▮ we're gonna be fine.

ZAID. We're gonna be ▮

35

Restaurant.

NEELAM. Zaid mentioned you've been working abroad a lot.

JEREMY. Mainly Berlin, teaching has been the bulk of it.

NEELAM. Haven't seen a play in so long.

JEREMY. Me neither. Well in the UK at least. How is anyone supposed to make art here in this economy?

NEELAM. Even law hasn't guaranteed an easy existence and that's with both me and Deji working.

Beat.

Did Zaid say how long he was going to be?

JEREMY. Five minutes, five minutes ago. He needs to hurry up. Have a plane to catch.

NEELAM. How has he been?

JEREMY. Throws himself into his work, but that's been pretty consistent since his dad.

NEELAM. And with his mum?

JEREMY. The worst of it was on the day he came out to her. But it's like a plaster, best to just rip it off as quickly as possible.

NEELAM. Don't know about that. My parents took ages to start properly speaking to me again.

JEREMY. To have to deal with that in this day and age.

NEELAM. They're fine now. What was it like when you came out?

JEREMY. Both my parents had been hippies. Was nervous of course but after the initial shock they were fine.

NEELAM. Lucky you.

JEREMY. Suppose.

    ZAID *enters*.

NEELAM. Congratulations!!

JEREMY. Yes, congratulations. Well done, darling!

ZAID. Thank you. Thank you.

NEELAM. Graduating and with a first. You smashed it.

ZAID. Sleeping with the lecturer might have helped.

JEREMY. Haven't been a lecturer there for over a year now, so might have been your own genius.

ZAID. My own genius then.

    ZAID *kisses* JEREMY.

    Beat.

NEELAM. Took loads of pictures.

ZAID. Always thought I'd get one with my mum and dad.

NEELAM. Sorry, Zaid.

ZAID. Need to save the melancholy because we're celebrating.

JEREMY. Well said.

NEELAM. I'll get us some drinks.

JEREMY. No, I need to run so I'm leaving my card behind the bar for you both.

NEELAM. You don't have to.

ZAID. Leaving already?

JEREMY. Been waiting half an hour and I have to get to Heathrow.

ZAID. Sorry, just seeing everyone from the course again and saying goodbye took ages.

JEREMY. Well, I'm back next weekend so you won't have to miss me too much.

They hug goodbye.

Lovely to see you too, Neelam.

NEELAM. Take care, Jeremy.

JEREMY *leaves.*

ZAID. And then there were two. It hasn't been the two of us in ages.

NEELAM. It's been a minute. Work has been full-on, more complex casework, which is great but I've also been sick.

ZAID. Nothing serious?

NEELAM. No, but that's why work was being shitty about today.

ZAID. Would have been too depressing to think of without at least some family here.

NEELAM. Did you even try to invite your mum?

ZAID. Yeah. She still won't take my calls.

NEELAM. Sorry.

ZAID. I thought by now... I don't know.

NEELAM. Give it time.

ZAID. Whatever happens I don't regret it, telling her. At least I got to tell one of my parents.

Silence.

NEELAM. Nice to see Jeremy.

ZAID. Yeah, don't know what I would have done without him. He's been a rock, really held me.

NEELAM. Great!

ZAID. Officially moved in as well. Got my own key and everything.

NEELAM. How is it living together?

ZAID. That bit's great. It's when he's away, there was always someone around at my mum's, not used to being by myself.

NEELAM. I can imagine.

ZAID. It's not all doom and gloom. I get plenty of time to write and hook-up.

NEELAM. You still doing that? Thought you both moving in together meant you'd got a bit more serious.

ZAID. We are serious, having an open relationship doesn't change that.

NEELAM. Okay. As long as you're happy.

ZAID. I am.

NEELAM. Great.

Silence.

ZAID. I actually have good news. They're putting my play on.

NEELAM. Fuck off.

ZAID. Very early days. Nothing signed yet.

NEELAM. That's amazing. Congratulations.

ZAID. Not going to lie, I am buzzed. It feels brilliant.

NEELAM. You, doing what we always wanted.

ZAID. Should have been you.

NEELAM. It was always meant to be you.

ZAID. Only took me till I was thirty-five.

NEELAM. At least you got there.

ZAID. Well it's not confirmed yet.

NEELAM. It will be.

ZAID. You don't ever get the urge to write now?

NEELAM. No. Prefer the black-and-white of the law. Writing
was all a different lifetime for me.

ZAID. It was the play you told me to write years ago.

NEELAM. What play?

ZAID. About a fifteen-year-old and an older guy.

Beat.

NEELAM. Right. And how has it been, writing it?

ZAID. Well, it's not my story, the characters are different. And
I've had the drama of coming out and Dad to overshadow
everything.

NEELAM. Of course.

ZAID. Just as I'm getting older I've been thinking more. I'm
getting closer to the age he was and well...

NEELAM. ...You would never, with a fifteen-year-old.

ZAID. Yeah.

NEELAM. Hope you're looking after yourself?

ZAID. You know me, resilient as fuck.

NEELAM. Proud of you.

ZAID. Thank you. You're the only person I've told by the way, so don't tell anyone. Don't want to jinx it.

NEELAM. I won't.

ZAID. Not even Jeremy.

NEELAM. You haven't told him?

ZAID. He's having a hard time of it. No one really wants to programme his stuff.

NEELAM. That's shit. I was never really a fan. But people loved his stuff.

ZAID. He's got it into his head to self-produce it.

NEELAM. Nice to be rich...

ZAID. Talking of Jeremy's money, think we should make the most of that tab behind the bar. What are you drinking?

NEELAM. Nothing for me.

ZAID. When have you ever turned down a free drink?

Beat.

NEELAM. I've got my own good news.

ZAID. Go on then. Don't hold back.

NEELAM. I'm pregnant.

ZAID. Right.

NEELAM. Zaid.

ZAID. What?

NEELAM. I think the word you're looking for is 'congratulations'.

ZAID. Of course, congratulations. I'm so happy for you.

NEELAM. Are you?

ZAID. Genuinely I am. Sorry, it just took me by surprise.

NEELAM. And that's the real reason for not being around much. It was a really rough first trimester.

ZAID. How far along are you?

NEELAM. Four-and-a-half months.

ZAID. How am I only finding out now?

NEELAM. Getting pregnant wasn't the easiest so I kept it to myself for ages and then I was nervous about telling you.

ZAID. Why?

NEELAM. For the exact reaction I got.

ZAID. I said I was just surprised.

NEELAM. It's me, Zaid. I know how you always look down on anyone with a kid.

ZAID. But you're not anyone.

    If I've ever made you feel that, I'm sorry. That was never my intention.

NEELAM. It's okay.

ZAID. How did your parents take it?

NEELAM. Happy their daughter is married and having a baby, finally. Yeah I never thought we'd get to this point.

ZAID. It's all worked out then.

NEELAM. Yeah.

ZAID, I am really fucking happy for you. You're gonna be a mum!

***

Jeremy's flat – JEREMY *enters.*

JEREMY. What are you still doing here?

ZAID. Just got a message from Neelam, she asked if we could reschedule.

JEREMY. So, you're not going out?

ZAID. No, her feet are too swollen, she had a kinda baby-shower thing yesterday and she overdid it.

JEREMY. Right and you weren't invited to that?

ZAID. It was just women.

JEREMY. And no gays?

ZAID. I know Neelam's been a bit rubbish recently, but it's not like that, there wouldn't be any men there.

JEREMY. Right.

ZAID. She wouldn't even have organised it.

JEREMY. Had a friend from school, Samantha. I was there through every boyfriend, nursed her through every heartbreak and then she got married. And that was it, apparently her husband felt uncomfortable with me around.

ZAID. Deji's fine with me.

JEREMY. It's not about who they're with, we just begin to not neatly fit into their lives.

ZAID. It's not the same. Okay? She's just pregnant.

JEREMY. Of course. Hey, why don't we do something then, while I'm in town.

ZAID. Fancy getting high and hitting a club?

JEREMY. Meant more like dinner.

Beat.

ZAID. Should probably just work.

JEREMY. If you want me to read anything or feed back, happy to.

ZAID. I'll let you know.

*****

Deji and Neelam's flat. DEJI *walks in.*

DEJI. He's asleep.

NEELAM. Should you leave him on his own? I'm going to go check on him.

DEJI. You've been with him all day. You need to rest too.

NEELAM. I'm fine.

DEJI. I'm going back in, just checking you're okay?

NEELAM. Yes. Actually, have you seen my phone? I should text people.

DEJI. Don't worry I've let the mums know he's here safe. And everyone else can wait.

DEJI *stares at* NEELAM *lovingly.*

NEELAM. Why are you looking at me like that?

DEJI. Like what?

NEELAM. Like you dropped a pill for the first time.

DEJI. You look beautiful.

NEELAM. You literally saw me shit myself and push a human out of my vagina. It was like having your insides ripped out.

DEJI. You were so brave.

NEELAM. I didn't have a choice.

DEJI. Didn't think it was possible for me to fall in love with you even more.

NEELAM. Stop it.

DEJI. Me, you and Adam.

NEELAM. Me, you and Adam. Now go make sure he's alright.

***

Phone.

ZAID. Hey, Neelam, congratulations!!! I got the message that Deji sent everyone. Adam? Pissed you didn't go with Zaid for the baby's name. You're probably recovering so just give me a shout when you're up to it and I'll come see you.

***

Deji and Neelam's house.

DEJI *and* NEELAM *together as they coo over the baby.*

***

Phone.

ZAID. Know you must be busy, but you get the flowers I sent? Did want to give them to you in person. So hopefully soon.

***

Phone.

NEELAM. Sorry for taking so long. Adam had jaundice, and then now he's not been sleeping. Thanks for the flowers. I need to give you a proper call, but come whenever.

***

Jeremy's flat.

JEREMY. Had lunch with an old pal today. Was hoping that he might be able to help with getting my play on.

ZAID. Any joy?

JEREMY. No. But he told me to pass on his congratulations.

ZAID. For what?

JEREMY. Your play. He tells me you have a play going on.

ZAID. Only just got full confirmation myself, I was going to tell you.

JEREMY. Once it was on?

ZAID. Was just waiting for the right time.

JEREMY. I'm delighted. Really delighted for you.

ZAID. Thanks.

Beat.

JEREMY. What did you think? I'd be mad with jealousy?

ZAID. No.

JEREMY. I would have been nothing but happy for you. I am nothing but happy for you. You're not the first of my former students to find success.

ZAID. I was just being sensitive to the situation.

JEREMY. Towards the washed-up old writer.

ZAID. No. You're none of those things.

JEREMY. They told me they don't need me in Berlin any more. 'Those who can do and those who can't teach.' So where does that leave me?

ZAID. I'm sorry.

JEREMY. This obsession with the new. The disregard for experience, for craft, for people like me.

ZAID. It'll turn around.

JEREMY. I'm not so sure, at one point or another every writer ends up where I am. You need to be an interesting perspective and that's what you have now. I've been lumbered in with the 'pale male and stale'. Everything I tried to counteract.

ZAID. Are you implying they only put on my play because I'm a brown queer person?

JEREMY. No

ZAID. I work hard.

JEREMY. We all work hard. It's good to remember everyone has their season.

ZAID. Maybe you should stop blaming the world. Write a play they can't say no to. That's what I did.

JEREMY. Maybe.

***

Phone.

ZAID. Hey I know you're busy but I didn't know who else to tell. Jeremy is being all funny about it. But I signed the contract. They're officially going to put on my play. I don't fucking believe it. I need someone to celebrate with. Call me when you get a chance. And how is baby?

***

Phone.

NEELAM. FUCKING CONGRATULATIONS!! That's such brilliant news. Adam's on a new formula. He's been puking a lot. I could do with a day off, so up for drinks, you around next week?

***

Phone.

ZAID. Yeah I'm defo around apart from Tuesday evening. Shall we say Wednesday?

***

Deji and Neelam's house.

NEELAM. My mum's sick too.

DEJI. So, she can't come?

NEELAM. I asked and I can't force her. Plus, who's going to pick her up

DEJI. Maybe you could ask someone else to come help? Zaid?

NEELAM. He's never been into kids.

DEJI. I thought he'd have been around more.

NEELAM. I suppose he's busy, he has a play on.

DEJI. Right. I could ask my mum?

NEELAM. Really don't need her seeing me and the flat in this state. You can't stay?

DEJI. I can't cancel.

NEELAM. I know it's work, but you know I was throwing up all last night.

DEJI. You said you were a bit better now.

NEELAM. I've not fucking slept.

DEJI. I have to be there.

NEELAM. And the baby's restless.

DEJI. When he's like this he clings to you.

Beat.

I'm sorry.

NEELAM. That's not good enough.

DEJI. I know, I know it really isn't. But I'm doing this for us. The family.

NEELAM. That fucking cliché.

DEJI. This is the hardest bit. Everyone says it, when he's a bit bigger and a bit more robust it'll all be easier.

The baby cries in the other room.

I'll do the night-feeds for the rest of the week. I swear.

NEELAM. And the nappies.

DEJI. And the nappies.

NEELAM. If I ever want another kid, you fucking shoot me.

***

Phone.

ZAID. I feel like we're a bit out of sync. So, looking forward to catching up. Will be good to reconnect.

***

Phone.

ZAID. Hey, I haven't heard back from you. Are we still doing Wednesday?

***

Phone.

ZAID. It's cool if you can't do Wednesday, just let me know either way?

***

ZAID *goes to message but just puts his phone back in his pocket.*

***

Jeremy's flat.

JEREMY. Are you working again this evening?

ZAID. Yes.

JEREMY. Thought we could spend some time together.

ZAID. Sorry, but I've got to rewrite.

JEREMY. Maybe I could help?

ZAID. I'm fine.

JEREMY. Well what do I know then.

ZAID. I'll go work in the bedroom.

JEREMY. I'm going to say yes to Austria.

ZAID. I can't have this conversation now.

JEREMY. I'm not going to stay here doing nothing.

ZAID. So you won't be here for when my play opens?

JEREMY. Unfortunately, no.

ZAID. And you're fine with that?

JEREMY. It's not like you have much time for me at the moment.

ZAID. What about the weeks I spent here on my own while you were off in Berlin?

JEREMY. I should be able to catch it before it finishes the run.

ZAID. Lucky me. And what about press night?

JEREMY. You can take someone else. Invite Neelam.

ZAID. Really?

JEREMY. Yeah.

ZAID. I need you. You of all people know how vulnerable this whole process is. How fucking exposed I feel right now. And this is the moment you choose to fuck off?

JEREMY. I couldn't say no. I need the work.

ZAID. You don't need the work. You've never needed the work.

JEREMY. It's more than the money.

ZAID. It's a fucking student production of your play.

JEREMY. Well, I'm sorry we can't all be main stage like you.

ZAID. And that's it, the real reason. Your petty jealousy.

JEREMY. That's not true.

ZAID. From the moment you found out about the play.

JEREMY. I think you're as much to blame for this awkwardness.

ZAID. No, Jeremy, this is all your jealousy.

JEREMY. I'm not jealous!

ZAID. Give me some other words then? What is it, envy? Resentment? Bitterness? I'm sorry I have a play on and you don't.

JEREMY. I've always been there for you, as much as I can. But this is hard for me, walking back into that theatre as your plus-one.

ZAID. And what is that if not jealousy?

JEREMY. I need you to understand this, Zaid, I really do.

ZAID. If you go then I won't be here when you come back.

JEREMY. That's up to you.

***

Club. High off their faces. An indie classic plays.

NEELAM. █████████████████

ZAID. ███████████████

NEELAM. ██████

ZAID. █████

█████████████████████

I love you. ██████████████████

NEELAM. ████████

ZAID. ████████████████████

NEELAM. ██████

ZAID. ████████████████████

████

NEELAM. ██████████████

ZAID. ██████████

NEELAM. ███████

ZAID. █████

NEELAM. ████████

█████████████████

████████████████

ZAID. ██████████████

36

Deji and Neelam's house.

DEJI. This is your first time at our new house, right?

ZAID. Yeah. It's lovely.

DEJI. We haven't seen you in ages.

ZAID. It's been a while.

DEJI. She finally convinced me to move east.

ZAID. Feels weird being back in the neighbourhood. Nothing's changed.

DEJI. You don't come back to see your family?

ZAID. No.

   Silence.

DEJI. Neelam tells me you're killing it, with the writing. Won an award.

ZAID. All very surreal.

DEJI. And they're putting it on again?

ZAID. Maybe.

DEJI. Brilliant, hopefully we'll get to see it this time.

   NEELAM *enters*

NEELAM. Sorry, took him longer to sleep than normal.

ZAID. Don't worry.

NEELAM. Overexcited. Meeting someone new.

DEJI. I'm going to leave you guys to it.

NEELAM. You don't have to.

DEJI. Nah, you two catch up.

   DEJI *exits.*

ZAID. Adam looks so much like you.

NEELAM. Do you think?

ZAID. Yes.

NEELAM. You're the only one who's said that.

ZAID. Your face shape and the eyes.

NEELAM. With my current bags, I hope not.

ZAID. You look great.

NEELAM. Real talk.

ZAID. You look great.

NEELAM. I'm a state. You're the one person who's supposed to keep it real.

ZAID. You're glowing, sure you're not pregnant again?

Awkward beat.

Sorry. I wasn't really asking. More of a joke.

NEELAM. It's just…

ZAID. Pretend I never said anything.

NEELAM. It's fine. Just early days… really early.

ZAID. Well… Congratulations.

NEELAM. Sooner than I expected, than we expected.

ZAID. Yeah. I've barely met this one.

NEELAM. Yeah, well. You've been busy.

ZAID. Me?

NEELAM. We've both been busy. But yours is a more glamorous busy.

ZAID. Don't know about that.

NEELAM. I wouldn't change it. But anything is more glamorous than endless nappies and moving house.

ZAID. Does it feel weird being back here?

NEELAM. Nice actually, slot right back in and useful having my mum around the corner to help with Adam.

ZAID. That's nice.

NEELAM. Yeah.

Silence.

Congratulations on the play.

ZAID. Thanks.

NEELAM. Sorry again I couldn't make it. Leaving Adam for that long was impossible.

ZAID. Right.

NEELAM. He was so clingy. Now it's all about Dad. He doesn't even want me to drop him to nursery.

ZAID. Did you read it?

NEELAM. It's just been so insane, going back to work and everything.

ZAID. Sent you a copy because you couldn't make it.

NEELAM. I know, I know, just haven't had the brain space to really sit and engage with anything.

Beat.

Saw the reviews, everyone seems to love it. You did it. Made it. Got what you wanted.

ZAID. My face was in *The Times* supplement and I couldn't find a place to stay.

NEELAM. What?

ZAID. In the middle of it all I was in-between places. After me and Jeremy broke up.

NEELAM. You should have called me.

ZAID. And said what? 'We haven't spoken properly in months but can I come and stay?'

NEELAM. Yeah that's exactly what you should have said.

ZAID. Honestly, wasn't sure you would pick up.

NEELAM. Life is busy when you have a kid, but you can always stay.

ZAID. You asked and I was being honest. I wasn't sure you would pick up. So, I didn't.

NEELAM. Where did you end up?

ZAID. Called Jeremy. He's actually been a good friend, a really good friend. Let me stay for a bit.

NEELAM. You're not back together are you?

ZAID. We've been talking about it.

NEELAM. You need to close that door.

ZAID. Why? I still love him. He still loves me.

Silence.

NEELAM. And are you staying with him now?

ZAID. I'm in a flatshare. At my age. Constantly think, was it worth it?

NEELAM. You stuck at it. You should be proud.

ZAID. Of what?

NEELAM. You have an award, you're in print, not everyone can say that.

ZAID. Not everyone can say they have a child with one on the way. Don't think I'll ever have a kid.

NEELAM. Do you even want one?

ZAID. Never thought it was even an option for someone like me. Been thinking about it more since my dad died. What my legacy is.

NEELAM. Right.

ZAID. You remember my dad died.

NEELAM. Of course I do. What do you mean by that?

ZAID. Nothing.

NEELAM. How is the rest of the family stuff?

ZAID. My mum responded to a birthday text, progress?

Beat.

NEELAM. You know you're always welcome here.

ZAID. Am I?

NEELAM. You know you are.

ZAID. And Deji would feel the same?

NEELAM. Of course. Why would you even ask that?

ZAID. Always got the feeling that he didn't like me very much.

NEELAM. Don't know where you would have got that from.

ZAID. Just a feeling. What about you?

NEELAM. What? Do I like you?

You're one of my best friends.

ZAID. Best friends don't have to catch each other up.

NEELAM. Life has just been busy.

ZAID. Friends are in each other's lives.

NEELAM. Like when your baby has to stay overnight in a phototherapy unit because he has jaundice.

ZAID. I didn't even know till after.

NEELAM. Maybe I didn't want to burden you with all my stuff. But you knew I was here, on my own, looking after a baby. How much did you come and visit?

ZAID. Like Rehana?

NEELAM. Really?

ZAID. See you on her Instagram a lot.

NEELAM. Yeah, Rehana lives local and it's useful to have another mum around.

ZAID. She treated you like shit the whole time we were at school.

NEELAM. We were kids. And she apologised for everything.

ZAID. I suppose people can change.

NEELAM. You're right, they do.

ZAID. And now you're best friends again.

NEELAM. Did you just hear yourself?

ZAID. Was I a back-up?

NEELAM. What?

ZAID. Was I just a back-up? For the family that didn't want to know, or the friends that never had the time. Until they did. Second choice?

NEELAM. No.

ZAID. Because you were my first choice. I chose you, and for someone like me that means something.

NEELAM. I love you, Zaid, but I have a family now. Other responsibilities. I'm not going to apologise for that. You're obviously going through a lot at the moment.

ZAID. Don't.

NEELAM. Zaid.

ZAID. Don't do that? Don't minimise this.

NEELAM. What do you want from me?

ZAID. I want this to hurt, as much as it does for me.

NEELAM. Stop being dramatic. This isn't one of your plays.

ZAID. How would you know? You've not even read it.

NEELAM. I did. I did read it and I couldn't finish it. You changed it, the guy who abused you was white and you changed his race.

ZAID. I wasn't abused, you don't get to decide that for me.

NEELAM. You made him a Pakistani guy.

ZAID. It's not my story, it's a play I wrote.

NEELAM. I said to myself I don't begrudge him selling out, who deserves a bit of success more than Zaid?

ZAID. That's what you got from reading my play? I put my heart in that play, made something from all the ugliness of everything that's gone on, and that's what you saw?

NEELAM. You asked and I told you the truth.

ZAID. If we're talking truths, ever since you got married I've been pushed further and further to the fringes of your life. Keep asking myself what is it about me that doesn't fit neatly into your new little world? I can only think of one thing.

NEELAM. And now you're trying to make this about you being gay? From day one I've always had your back.

ZAID. But that changed. When it meant actually putting something at stake to have me at the table.

NEELAM. What are you talking about?

ZAID. Racism is bad, but homophobia is fine. I fought for you and Deji, but you? You were happy to just disregard me.

NEELAM. That's not true, just because my world changed, doesn't make me homophobic.

ZAID. There should have been a place for me in that world. Chosen me like I would have chosen you.

NEELAM. Really? You would have chosen me, like I am? Like I am now? The disdain for my life choices radiates off you. Maybe that's why it's difficult to be around you.

ZAID. And what about you and your constant judgements of me and Jeremy?

NEELAM. Me? You hate the fact that I'm 'basic' and happy.

ZAID. I never called you that.

NEELAM. You didn't need to. You will never accept I don't want what you have.

ZAID. You could have had it and more.

NEELAM. What don't you understand? I love my life.

ZAID. You can lie to yourself, but I know the real you.

NEELAM. No you don't, Zaid, you haven't known me for a long time.

Silence.

ZAID. Do you remember when you came up to see me at uni the night I came out to you?

NEELAM. Yeah.

ZAID. That must have been over fifteen years ago now. I was so scared. You were the first person in my life I'd told I was gay. Then we were high on that dance floor. In that moment I looked at you, overcome by this feeling, and it wasn't the drugs, it was this feeling of certainty. That it didn't matter what would come next, because you'd be there. You'd always be there.

No one has ever got me like you do.

Beat.

NEELAM. Life hadn't come for us yet.

After a while, ZAID *gets up.*

ZAID. Take care, Neelam.

NEELAM. Take care, Zaid.

ZAID *exits.*

*****

Club. High off their faces. An indie classic plays.

NEELAM. Can you feel anything?

ZAID. Yeah. Yeah. Can you?

NEELAM. Yeah.

ZAID. Yeah!

They both uncontrollably laugh.

I love you. Like genuinely I love you.

NEELAM. I love you too.

ZAID. No really, I love the bones of you.

NEELAM. What?

ZAID. I LOVE THE BONES OF YOU.

Beat.

NEELAM. I love the skin of you.

ZAID. The teeth of you.

NEELAM. The eyes.

ZAID. The ears.

NEELAM. The nose.

A moment of intense connection.

You know we're gonna be fine.

ZAID. We're gonna be fucking brilliant.

They dance and it's perfect and life is yet to come for them but it will.

The End.

A Nick Hern Book

The Real Ones first published in Great Britain in 2024 as a paperback original by Nick Hern Books Limited, The Glasshouse, 49a Goldhawk Road, London W12 8QP, in association with the Bush Theatre, London

Cover photography by Laurie Fletcher

Designed and typeset by Nick Hern Books, London
Printed in Great Britain by Mimeo Ltd, Huntingdon, Cambridgeshire PE29 6XX

A CIP catalogue record for this book is available from the British Library

ISBN 978 1 83904 386 4

www.nickhernbooks.co.uk/environmental-policy